PEARLS TAKES
A WRONG TURN

Other *Pearls Before Swine* Collections

Treasuries

Gift Books

Kids' Books

PEARLS TAKES A WRONG TURN

Stephan
PASTIS

A *PEARLS BEFORE SWINE* TREASURY

Andrews McMeel
PUBLISHING®

Pearls Before Swine is distributed internationally by Andrews McMeel Syndication.

Pearls Takes a Wrong Turn copyright © 2018 by Stephan Pastis. All rights reserved. Printed in China. No part of this book may be used or reproduced in any manner whatsoever without written permission except in the case of reprints in the context of reviews.

Andrews McMeel Publishing
a division of Andrews McMeel Universal
1130 Walnut Street, Kansas City, Missouri 64106

www.andrewsmcmeel.com

18 19 20 21 22 SDB 10 9 8 7 6 5 4 3 2 1

ISBN: 978-1-4494-8936-6

Library of Congress Control Number: 2018932951

Pearls Before Swine can be viewed on the internet at www.pearlscomic.com.

These strips appeared in newspapers from September 7, 2015, to March 11, 2017.

Editor: Lucas Wetzel
Creative Director: Tim Lynch
Photographer: Thomas Gibson
Cover, Inside Cover Art: Donna Oatney
Title Design: Holly Swayne
Text Design: Spencer Williams
Production Manager: Chuck Harper

Production Editor: Amy Strassner
Prop and Wardrobe Stylist: Sher Gibson
Assistant and Location Scout: Jon Demonte
Image Composite: Graphics Four
Cover Model: Jenna Kaufman
Hair and Makeup: Mary Stewart
Location: Kansas City, Missouri

Dedication

To my son, Thomas.
You grew up way too fast.
Please reverse this if you can.
Also, answer my texts.

Introduction

I was two miles above sea level and about to puke.

It was altitude sickness.

And before going to Cusco, Peru (to see the nearby Inca fortress of Machu Picchu), I had been warned about it. Warned to take special pills that mitigate the effect.

But I hadn't.

And now my head was throbbing. My arm hurt. I was dizzy. And I was nauseous.

So I lay down in bed and tried to pass the time by emailing people, including my daughter, Julia, back in California.

> **From: pearlscomic@gmail.com**
> **To:** *(my daughter)*
> **Date: Sun, October 8, 2017**
>
> **Hi! I'm two miles above you in the Andes. Altitude makes your head hurt. And ten stairs makes you out of breath.**
>
> **But I'm in Cusco!**

Then I tried to sleep. But no luck.

So I looked at stuff on my phone, checked the internet, looked at sports scores.

And at 5:17 a.m., I got an email from my daughter that will forever be seared into my brain.

> **From:** *(my daughter)*
> **To: pearlscomic@gmail.com**
> **Date: Mon, October 9, 2017**
>
> **There is a massive fire here.**
> **We have evacuated and are safe.**
> **We don't know if the house or condo are going to make it.**

"Here" would be my hometown of Santa Rosa, California.

The "house" is where we live. The "condo" is where I draw.

And the two buildings are not next to each other.

They are two miles apart.

I didn't know what to think. Was it a weird joke? And if it wasn't, how could there be a fire that stretched for two miles?

So I wrote back.

Eloquently.

> **From: pearlscomic@gmail.com**
> **To:** *(my daughter)*
>
> **What??**

But she didn't respond. And so I immediately called my wife, Staci.

And it was no joke.

My hometown was burning down.

She and Julia were huddled together in a parking lot that had been turned into an evacuation center. They were safe, but it looked like our home was not.

There were so many fires that night that firemen just could not keep up. Two of those fires were headed toward our house. And there were no firemen left to fight them.

So the entire neighborhood just to the north of us caught fire. Almost every single one of the homes was burning.

On my phone, I was able to find live coverage of the fires on one of the local San Francisco news stations. All the structures they were showing—two hotels, a mobile home lot, and a Kmart—were all just down the hill from our house.

I wanted to come home immediately. My wife didn't want me to. We argued.

She said it was better that I stay there. Our neighborhood had been evacuated and she and Julia would be staying at an aunt's house. I would just be one more person needing a bed. I argued that I couldn't stay on the trip. But she won. And I stayed.

And I just sat there in my rented Cusco house watching the coverage. Obsessively staring at a map of the fires. Seeing them surround my house.

For two straight days.

And in the midst of all of this was Machu Picchu. The very reason I went to Peru. And just a few hours away from Cusco.

"Go," my wife kept saying during our many phone calls. "It's why you went there. What happens to the house happens. Go and see it."

It felt absurd. Being a tourist while my neighborhood was burning. But I was going crazy watching the fires on my phone. And I hadn't left the house in two days.

So I went, along with my cousin Vincent, who had come with me on the trip.

And after a long bus ride to the top of the mountain, we got to Machu Picchu.

And as beautiful as it is, high up there in the clouds, it is not the world's safest place. Stairs don't have railings. Steps are uneven. And if you fall, you will fall thousands of feet. And it will not be pleasant.

So I climbed the first set of stairs and stopped and turned to my cousin.

"Dude, I can't do it."

"What's wrong?" he asked.

"I'm a wreck. I'm dizzy. I'm scared. And I can't stop thinking about my house."

"What do you want to do?" he asked.

"I'll just go to the café or something," I told him. "Take as much time seeing it as you want. I'll just wait for you down here."

So he hugged me. And I went to a little café at the base.

And there I just cried.

I was sitting at a long communal table, and I can only imagine what the strangers across from me thought. Surely, I was ruining their Machu Picchu experience as well.

And with the little bit of charge I had left on my phone, I called my daughter.

"I love you, and I miss you," I told her. "My phone's about to die, but I just wanted to hear your voice."

"I love you, too," she said. "How is Machu Picchu?"

"Bad," I said. "Horrible. I'm just so worried."

"Don't worry," she said. "We're okay. It's just the house and your studio we're not sure about. But we're fine."

So I hung up and a couple hours later met my cousin. And we left Machu Picchu.

In the days that followed, the extent of damage to my hometown became known.

4,600 houses were gone. Including our previous home where I had drawn *Pearls* for almost ten years.

And so my trip to Peru ended. And I flew home. And when I got to Santa Rosa, I couldn't believe what I was seeing.

Our old neighborhood:

And our old house—with the only recognizable feature being a chess set we had built in our backyard (lower left):

But somehow, some way, our present house, just a few miles to the south, was still standing.

Embers had fallen everywhere, like in the cushion of an upstairs balcony chair, but through a miracle of God, they had not ignited.

And while the fire had gotten within two blocks, it had not taken our house.

And the condo where I draw was okay, too.

In the months that followed, the clearance of debris began, a process still going on as I write this. And my wife and I helped put together a fundraiser for the victims. And our city began the long process of recovery.

And in January, because I am the most restless human you will ever meet, I went off again on another one of my trips, telling my daughter to not let the town burn down this time.

I went again with my cousin Vincent (no one else will travel with me). And this time we went to Mexico City.

Mostly because I wanted to see the giant pyramids of Teotihuacán.

One of them, the Pyramid of the Sun, is one of the largest in the world, over 200 feet high.

And when I got to see it in person and stood at the base, it was incredible to see:

Though the stairs were a bit more steep than I expected (see photo on right).

And that's when I realized that my fear of climbing Machu Picchu was about more than just the fire.

I was afraid of heights.

Specifically, steep stairs.

Where I can fall.

And the Rat and Pig would be no more.

"You go up," I told my cousin Vincent. "I'm gonna stay down here."

"You sure?" he asked, endlessly patient with the cousin who doesn't like high places.

"Yeah, I'm sure."

So off he went, and I stayed at the base.

And as I stared up at the pyramid, something happened.

That pyramid somehow became a symbol. Of something I had to overcome. A stupid fear.

And it brought back Machu Picchu. And how my memory of it was forever tainted by the fire. And what I wasn't able to do.

But we had survived that fire. And I was standing at the foot of this great pyramid, and I probably wasn't ever going to be here again.

So I started climbing.

The slowest man on the structure.

Oh, not upright. But on all fours. My hands clutching the stairs ahead. I was passed by kids, obese people, and one old woman with a cane.

The woman stared at me as I climbed on all fours and gave me a look you reserve for someone having a stroke.

"Are you okay?" she asked. "Do you need help?"

I wanted to tell her that indeed I was having a stroke. Because it sounded so much better than "I'm just scared. You keep going up the mountain, you very old woman with one good leg."

But instead I told her I was fine. And kept moving.

I paused at each landing and just tried to control my breathing, my heart about to pound its way out of my chest.

And 200 feet later, there were no more stairs to climb.

And I stood upright and looked around and could see everything, including the smaller Pyramid of the Moon below.

And then I saw my cousin.

"You climbed up! You made it!" he said, hugging me.

"Yeah," I answered. "I made it."

Stephan Pastis
October 2018

Panel 1: LOOK AT ME, GOAT... I'VE BECOME A JUDGE. IT'S ALWAYS BEEN A LIFE-LONG DREAM OF MINE.

Panel 2: GOOD FOR YOU, RAT. THAT'S A CRITICAL ROLE IN OUR SYSTEM OF DUE PROCESS. WHAT MADE YOU WANT TO DO IT?

Panel 3: THEY GIVE YOU A HAMMER TO HIT IDIOTS.

Panel 4: THAT'S NOT WHAT THAT'S FOR. OKAY, YOU'RE FIRST.

I was a lawyer in San Francisco for almost ten years. While I was never hit with a hammer, I did have another lawyer throw a microphone at me. He missed.

Panel 1: HEY, RAT, WHAT ARE YOU DOING? I'M A JUDGE NOW. I'M THE LIVING EMBODIMENT OF JUSTICE.

Panel 2: WHAT'S ON YOUR DESK THERE? A TIP JAR. THE MORE YOU PUT IN IT, THE MORE JUSTICE-Y I FEEL.

Panel 3: SO *THAT'S* HOW JUSTICE WORKS. YOU GET WHAT YOU PAY FOR.

Panel 1: I HEARD YOU HAD TO TEACH PIG ALL ABOUT WINE. YEAH, HE'S GOING TO A FANCY RESTAURANT WITH PIGITA AND WANTS TO IMPRESS HER WITH HIS WINE KNOWLEDGE.

Panel 2: SO NOW HE KNOWS HOW TO ORDER A GOOD BOTTLE AND TASTE THE LITTLE SAMPLE THAT THE WAITER BRINGS YOU? YEAH. THOUGH THERE'S JUST ONE LITTLE STEP I'M WORRIED ABOUT.

Panel 3: MUST YOU USE A SWIRLY STRAW?

Fun Stephan Fact: I do not like wine. And yet I live in the wine country of Northern California. I should move to beer country, wherever that is.

This was loosely premised on a famous case where a woman who spilled hot coffee on herself sued McDonald's for a lot of money and won. After the strip ran, I was surprised to get angry feedback from readers who said that the woman's case had more merit than is commonly understood. I don't know if they were right or wrong. But I do know that I got bored and deleted their emails.

If you look really closely at the last panel, you'll see that there is a cross on the book the woman is holding, meaning that this is a Christian church, and not a mosque or a synagogue. Or, if it is a mosque or a synagogue, she's a heretic. Either way, it's details like that that make me the revered cartoonist I am.

9/13

I think this was the hardest pun I ever wrote, mostly because the song lyric quoted is so long.

I'm often tempted to have the *Pearls* characters made into sculptures that I could put around my yard. It would be a very vain thing to do. And that's why I like the idea.

I draw a mean halberd, if that's what the thing the cat's holding is called. I do know for certain that the other thing the cat is holding is called a "rope."

I was sued for the first time in my life a couple weeks ago. Because deer ate a neighbor's fruit tree. But I don't own any deer. So the trial should be interesting.

Larry is wrong. The top surface of the memorial is sloped, and his beer would fall off. #Neverspillyourbrew

I just realized that Rat's eye mask, which appears in Panel 3, never appears again. This is what is known in the business as a "continuity error." A better cartoonist would not have committed it.

In 1979, I was 11. And while I was not hurt by a girl, I was hurt by the Seven Dwarfs. And that's because I had a plastic set of them, and my friend Emilio and I used to pull off their heads and throw them as hard as we could at each other.

I took four years of Spanish in high school, and on a recent trip to Peru, I finally put it to good use. I had no choice, as there were many cities where people spoke only Spanish. And I did not speak it well, as there were many words I mixed up like *sentar* (to sit) and *sentir* (to feel). So more than once I tried to tell someone to seat themselves and ended up telling them to feel themselves.

Panel 1: LISTEN, GOAT, I'VE TAKEN TO HEART WHAT YOU SAID ABOUT LEADING A MORE EXCITING, FULFILLING LIFE.

Panel 2: GOOD FOR YOU, TIMMY THE TORTOISE. HAVE YOU DECIDED TO FINALLY COME OUT OF YOUR SHELL AND SEE THE WORLD? MEET NEW PEOPLE? HAVE SOME ADVENTURES?

Panel 4: SATELLITE T.V. IS NOT— / PIPE DOWN. SPORTSCENTER'S ON.

I drew that satellite dish so well in the third panel that I went ahead and cut-and-pasted it into the fourth panel. That's what we in the business call "lazy."

Panel 1: I'M STAYING AT A CHARMING LITTLE BED AND BREAKFAST NEXT WEEK. / WHAT'S A BED AND BREAKFAST?

Panel 2: WELL, THEY VARY, OF COURSE, BUT IN GENERAL, THEY'RE —

Panel 3: SOME WEIRDO'S HOUSE WHERE YOU EAT WITH STRANGERS AND SOMETIMES FIND THEM IN YOUR BATHROOM.

Panel 4: I NEED MY BATHROOM ALONE-TIME! / THEY'RE NOT IN YOUR BATHROOM. / IT'S LIKE HELL, BUT WITHOUT THE FLAMES.

I recently tried to stay at an Airbnb in Tennessee. The owner was this really strange, short woman. And when she toured me through the house, she spent 15 minutes going through each box of cereal that she had. That scared me. So I fled and stayed at a hotel.

Panel 1: WHAT ARE YOU DOING, RAT? / I GOT A JOB WRITING SCHOLARLY FILM CRITICISM. CHECK OUT MY FIRST MOVIE REVIEW.

Panel 2: Someone should hit the director with a stick.

Panel 3: I TAKE IT YOU DIDN'T LIKE IT. / I DUNNO. I HAVEN'T SEEN IT.

LONELY LINDY WAS LONELY.

SO SHE WENT ON FACEBOOK TO FIND OLD HIGH SCHOOL CLASSMATES.

AND LOOKED UP THE SKINNY DEBATE GEEK AND THE PIMPLY TUBA PLAYER AND THE SWEATY YEARBOOK EDITOR...

AND BROCK ROCKSON.

HIGH SCHOOL QUARTERBACK, BLOND-HAIRED STUD, AND MUSCLED ADONIS, BROCK'S PROFILE PHOTO WAS THE LOGO OF THE DETROIT LIONS.

'HE MUST HAVE GONE ON TO BE A PRO QUARTERBACK,' LINDY THOUGHT, AS SHE SENT BROCK A FACEBOOK MESSAGE.

'HI, I'M LINDY,' SHE SAID. 'I WENT TO HIGH SCHOOL WITH YOU. WOULD YOU EVER WANT TO GET COFFEE?' AND TO HER SURPRISE, BROCK SAID YES.

9/27

AND ON THE DAY OF THE MEETING, LINDY MADE HERSELF AS BEAUTIFUL AS POSSIBLE FOR HER HIGH SCHOOL ADONIS.

WHO SHOWED UP AN HOUR LATE.

SORRY. WAS GAMBLING ON THE PONIES. YOU LINDY?

LINDY DELETED HER FACEBOOK ACCOUNT AND SET FIRE TO HER COMPUTER.

DON'T LOOK BACK. SOMEONE MIGHT BE CHANGING ON YOU.

How did Lindy, who has no neck in Panels 1 through 7, suddenly grow a neck in Panel 8? We'll never know.

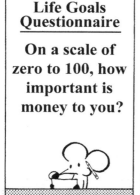

This was a really popular strip.

Okay, I really want to know the answer to this. Because I have a Honda Accord, and it really does have a speedometer that goes up that high. Could it really go that fast? Do they want me to experiment?

24

One of the Supremes apparently liked this strip and, through a friend, asked me for the original. No Supreme Court justices asked me for anything.

I'm hoping that "Togetherness makes the heart more annoyed" catches on. So far, Hallmark hasn't called.

When a strip has a whole lot of panels, like this one, I often get rid of some of the panel lines because it gives me a little bit of extra space to draw. And if that's not the kind of compelling information people love, I don't know what is.

Squirrels are inherently funny. As are pants. And cheese. Some things just cannot be explained.

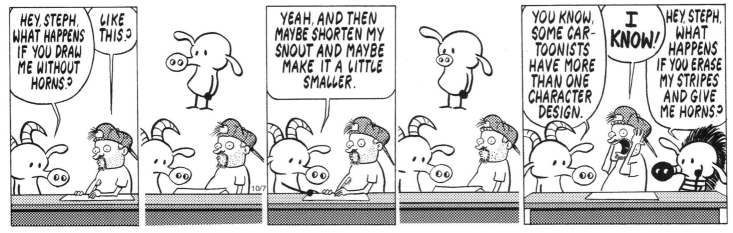

Darn. I've given away my secret formula.

27

RAT AND PIG HAVE FOUND A MONEY TREE

OKAY, PIG, NOW THAT WE'VE FOUND THE MONEY TREE, WE HAVE TO GUARD AGAINST ANYONE ELSE FINDING IT, BUT IN A SMART, SUBTLE WAY THAT DOESN'T AROUSE SUSPICION.

HEY GUYS, WHAT ARE YOU — WHOA, IS THAT MONEY UP—

CRACK

REMEMBER — HE GOT HIT BY A VERY LARGE COCONUT.

CHECK IT OUT, GOAT...I'M MAKING BABY DOLLS FOR KIDS. IN FACT, I'M SELLING SO MANY I CAN'T KEEP UP AND DON'T KNOW WHAT TO DO.

ASK AROUND HERE AT THE CAFE. I'M SURE THERE ARE TONS OF PEOPLE WHO NEED WORK.

PARDON ME, MA'AM, BUT WOULD YOU LIKE TO MAKE BABIES WITH ME?

NO ONE NEEDS WORK.

Those are some frightening-looking babies.

AT WHAT POINT DOES A HOME REPAIR PROJECT BECOME TOO BIG AND TOO COMPLEX FOR YOU, SUCH THAT YOU FEEL THE NEED TO CALL IN A REPAIR PROFESSIONAL?

IF IT INVOLVES A HAMMER.

NOT THE HANDY TYPE?

OR IF THE BATTERY COVER FALLS OFF THE REMOTE.

This is me. I cannot fix a single thing. Nothing. I am, for the most part, useless.

We require people to pass a test in order to become a citizen. So why don't we do the same thing for someone who wants to vote? Shouldn't you have to know some basic things before we let you determine the course of our country? Or, maybe just let *me* run everything. I'm pretty smart. Except when it comes to fixing things.

When I go to my daughter's high school tennis matches, I sometimes boo. It makes me laugh. Though I think some of the other parents find it odd.

I'd like to act like I know what all those words in the second panel mean. But I don't. So maybe I shouldn't be running the country after all.

Ah, Bill O'Reilly, a man who no longer has a job due to various sexual harassment scandals. The first of many men to fall from grace in 2017.

I sometimes hear from a couple of my high school English teachers after strips like this run. I don't think they're thrilled with me.

Angry Bob was angry.

"I will fly to Las Vegas and that will make me happy."

Near the end of the flight, the flight attendant made an announcement.

"We've begun our descent. But before we land, I thought we'd have some fun with a game I call, 'Get to Know Your Fellow Passengers.'"

"Here's how it works: One person will speak and say their favorite thing about this trip to Vegas. Then the next person will say hi to the previous person and say *their* favorite thing about this trip."

"I'll go first," said the flight attendant. "My name is Katy. I like the Vegas hotels." A flight attendant named Jack stood up next. "Hi, Katy. The casinos."

10/18

Angry Bob, excited by how much fun he was having on the flight, stood up next.

"Hi, Jack! This airplane!"

T.S.A. officials arrested Bob upon arrival.

FUN IS OVERRATED.

The return of Angry Bob! He used to be a fairly regular part of my Sunday strips, but he sort of disappeared for ten or so years. So I thought I'd bring him back. In most strips, he achieves some brief moment of happiness or awareness and then dies, usually violently.

I'M LEARNING HOW TO TURN WOOD INTO PAPER. / **WHO'S TEACHING YOU?**

A PRIEST. HE TEACHES ME RIGHT FROM THE PULPIT. AND HE USES VISUAL AIDS LIKE PUPPETS TO MAKE IT EASIER TO UNDERSTAND. / **WHAT ARE YOU TWO TALKING ABOUT?**

PIG'S A PULPIT PUPPET PULPING PUPIL.

I SHALL BEAT YOU TO A PULP.

HEY, GOAT. WHATCHA DOING TODAY? / **HE'S TAKING A BATH WITH HUNDREDS OF MARGINALLY CLEAN STRANGERS.**

I'M GOING SWIMMING AT THE PUBLIC POOL.

I THINK I SAID THAT.

I sort of share Rat's reaction to public pools. It really is like taking a bath with strangers.

WHERE'S RAT TODAY? / **HOSTAGE NEGOTIATION CLASS. HE WANTS TO LEARN HOW THE POLICE DO IT.**

WHAT DO THEY TEACH THEM? / **WELL, I THINK THE FIRST CLASS IS JUST FINDING OUT HOW YOU'D NATURALLY REACT TO A FRIEND OF YOURS BEING TAKEN HOSTAGE.**

WE NEVER LIKED HIM MUCH ANYWAYS!! / **OKAY.. UH.. NOT IDEAL.**

Maybe it's me, but I don't think I'd negotiate for the return of some people. I'd just wish them well and say, "Better luck next time."

I sometimes wonder how I get away with this stuff.

Just between us friends, the word I have in mind there is "sh*t." And that's the kind of inside knowledge that gives these treasuries so much added value.

10/25

Speaking of which, I am on Twitter! My Twitter handle is @stephanpastis. I often use it to offer signed books. Plus, I'm very, very amusing.

If I had to sum up my 16-year cartooning career to date, I would sum it up as follows: I got better at drawing toilets.

The internet. Neatly explained in one little comic strip.

Give yourself two *Pearls* points if you knew what the *Monitor* and the *Merrimack* were without looking it up. Give yourself more points if you cheated and looked it up.

Tom Seaver was one of the greatest pitchers in the history of baseball. And one day while I was writing the strip at a café in Calistoga, California, he walked in. I thought that was pretty cool.

RAT CHANNELS THE SPIRIT OF RUBE GOLDBERG
SORT OF

Stephan (A) tells a bad pun that nobody likes.

(A)

Causing reader (B) to throw newspaper in disgust.

(B)

Hitting a random dog. (c)

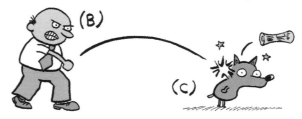
(c)

Who gets angry and bites the leg of a random flute player. (D)

CRUNCH
(D)

Causing the flute to hit a very high note. (E)

(E)

That distracts two drivers (F), both named Burt, who crash into each other and die.

(F)

Which Stephan reads about in a newspaper, giving him an idea. (G)

(G)

About killing two Burts with one tone. (H)

(H)

11/1

Fun Fact: I went to Elvis's home Graceland three times in one year. And I'm not even an Elvis fan. I can't explain that.

I'm proud to say that I could not name a single judge on *American Idol*. So I had to look that one up.

Doing a strip that mentions turmoil in the Middle East is guaranteed to be timely, no matter when it runs.

This confused a lot of readers. It was a pun on what LeBron James said when he left the Cleveland Cavaliers to play for the Miami Heat ("I'm going to take my talents to South Beach"). I thought everyone knew the quote. But I was wrong.

On a recent trip to Washington, D.C., I got to tour the Pentagon, courtesy of a *Pearls* fan who works there. The huge building surrounds a central courtyard, where normal-looking people just sit and eat their lunch. I was expecting something much more sinister.

11/8

Any similarity to Comcast Cable is purely coincidental.

My toilet drawing just gets better and better.

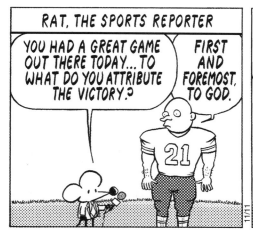

If the winning team gives credit to God for the win, should the losing team blame him? It would be fun to hear an athlete try.

I'M HERE WITH OUR FOOTBALL ANALYST, TRENT. TRENT, WHAT'S THE KEY TO TODAY'S GAME?

RAT, THE KEY TODAY WILL BE SCORING POINTS.

GOOD, TRENT. SCORING POINTS SEEMS TO BE AN INTEGRAL PART OF WINNING A FOOTBALL GAME. WHICH RAISES ANOTHER QUESTION...DOES SOMEONE ACTUALLY PAY YOU FOR THIS?

THIS IS NOT GOING WELL.

SO, TRENT, WILL SHOWING UP FOR THE GAME BE ANOTHER KEY?

I watch a lot of sports, and the announcer's "keys to the game" are almost always this glib.

WHY DOES JEF THE CYCLIST ALWAYS HAVE TO WEAR SPANDEX?

I GUESS HE THINKS SPANDEX IS FLATTERING TO THE HUMAN BODY.

WELL, GUESS WHO TOOK UP CYCLING.

MY EYES CAN'T UN-SEE THAT.

IF ONLY STACI COULD SEE ME NOW.

ARE YOU CYCLING WITH CHILD?

I look pregnant here. I am not pregnant.

DO YOU EVER WISH YOU HAD MORE FRIENDS?

WHAT FOR?

FRIENDS BROADEN YOUR KNOWLEDGE, TEACH YOU NEW STUFF, SHOW YOU AROUND NEW PLACES.

YOU JUST DESCRIBED GOOGLE.

SEARCH ENGINES AREN'T FRIENDS.

I'D SAY WE'RE BESTIES.

After I colored this Sunday, it dawned on me that I may have done this exact same joke before. But by then it was too late. So I pretended not to know.

One time while doing a signing for soldiers at a base in Afghanistan, a female soldier came up to my table. I asked her if she wanted me to sign something. She said, "No, my sergeant just told me I had to sit here." Never assume.

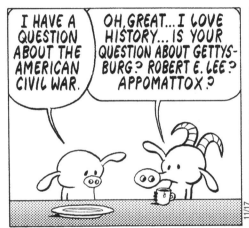

One time I had to sign 5,000 *Timmy Failure* books at a warehouse in Westminster, Maryland. During the lunch break, I hopped in my rental car and toured Gettysburg. But I was in a such a hurry that I drove the wrong way on a one-way road around the battlefield. Many people got angry that day.

I once went to a diner in Savannah, Georgia, with *FoxTrot* creator Bill Amend. Bill ordered pancakes. That's only mildly related to this strip, but I couldn't think of what else to say.

I don't know if this really works with babies, but I know it works with bulldogs. My friend had one, and when I would walk with him in Hermosa Beach, California, lots of women came up to talk to him.

This one is based on a Bob Dylan lyric ("How many roads must a man walk down before you call him a man?"). Dylan is my all-time favorite artist.

Ironically, I now write kids books (the *Timmy Failure* series). They do not contain stalkers.

Bonus *Pearls* points to any of you who noticed they are making a puzzle of another character, Snuffles the cat.

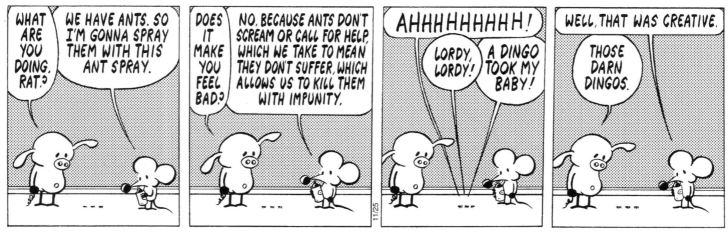

I think there is a lot of truth in this. We wouldn't do it if they screamed. Ants should learn how to scream.

One time in grade school we had to do a report on any animal. I chose the warthog, because it was the ugliest animal in the book. I should see a therapist.

Now and then people will surprise me and say they want me to bring the warthog character back. I never know which characters people will like.

49

One of the things I love most about traveling in foreign countries is that I rarely use my cell phone (because I'm too lazy to get an international plan). But the result is this great feeling of always being in the moment, always being present. And that's the most touchy-feely I will get in the course of this commentary.

"Significant other" has to be one of the most awkward phrases around. Makes me want to meet the "insignificant" one.

Pig says that Rat is returning from a vacation, presumably a long one, as he is making a sign welcoming him home. But there is no reference anywhere else in the prior week's strips to Rat being gone. In fact, he was in the Sunday strip just three days prior. This is a long way of saying continuity is for losers.

This 3-1-1 number really does exist. And I'm sure that at least one reader called it to ask Rat's question. I wonder what answer they got.

I'm fairly confident that on the days I reference Benito Mussolini I am the only comic strip author doing so.

Comic Strip Tip: If you do a comic strip like this, be prepared for a lot of emails that read thusly:

"Yesterday's strip befuddled me! I simply don't understand it."

All I did was hide a bunch of states within the strip. They are Nevada, Wyoming, Colorado, South Carolina, Michigan, Maine, Pennsylvania, West Virginia, and Washington.

PARDON ME, SIR, BUT YOUR NUMBER IS UP.

OHHH, GAWWWD!! I'M TOO YOUNG!! I HAVE A WIFE!! AND KIDS!! OHH GAWWWD!!!

MAYBE NEXT TIME I'LL COME TO THE DELI ALONE.

YOU GONNA GET YOUR SANDWICH OR NOT, PAL?

NOW SERVING 61

I know what you're thinking: What is the significance of the number 61 that is now being served? Short answer: None, because I just noticed it now.

MAKE ME FEEL BETTER, PIG. MY EX-WIFE IS DATING ONE CLOWN AFTER ANOTHER.

AW, STEPH. THAT'S PROBABLY NOT A NICE THING TO SAY.

THANK YOU, RONALD... I HAD A WONDERFUL NIGHT.

SHE'S A SUCKER FOR A HAPPY MEAL.

My wife is still with me. So the only clown she is dating is me.

DID YOU KNOW THAT FOUR BABIES ARE BORN EVERY SECOND?

WHERE'D YOU READ THAT?

BOOM. OUT POP EIGHT BABIES.

WHAT?

BOOM. OUT POP FOUR MORE.

AH. I SEE WHAT YOU'RE DOING. SO I'M GONNA TAKE A COUPLE MINUTES TO USE THE RESTROOM AND WHEN I COME BACK, MAYBE YOU'LL BE DONE.

AND THERE'LL BE 480 NEW BABIES!!

WILL THEY BE COMMUTING ON MY FREEWAY?

HI, PIG...I'D LIKE YOU TO MEET MY FRIEND, BRIAN....HE DESIGNS THE AUTOCORRECT FEATURE FOR ALL THE TEXTS PEOPLE SEND.

THAT SEEMS SO COMPLEX. HOW DO YOU KNOW WHAT WORD TO CHANGE IT TO?

I FIND THE MOST EMBARRASSING AND PICK THAT.

THAT SEEMS UNFAIR.

PROGRAMMERS NEED JOY IN THEIR LIVES, ALSO!

"Autocorrect fails." Google it.

DO YOU FORGIVE AND FORGET THE BAD THINGS PEOPLE DO TO YOU?

YES. I FORGIVE PEOPLE ALL THE TIME.

BUT I NEVER FORGET DIDDLY!!

NEVER MIND.

REMEMBERING IS THE FIRST STEP TO EXACTING VENGEANCE.

As I get older, I find it easier to forgive and forget. Not because I'm getting kinder, but because my memory is getting worse.

WITH ALL THE OVERPOPULATION IN THE WORLD, WHAT IF WE MADE A RULE THAT COUPLES CAN HAVE NO MORE THAN TWO CHILDREN?

WHY TWO?

BECAUSE THAT ALLOWS THE COUPLE TO REPLICATE ONLY THEMSELVES. AND BESIDES, NO FAMILY'S THIRD CHILD HAS EVER CONTRIBUTED ANYTHING WORTHWHILE TO THIS WORLD.

I KNOW YOU KNOW I'M A THIRD CHILD.

I REITERATE MY POSITION.

GEE, MAYBE TWO SHOULD BE THE RULE.

I have two older sisters, Penny and Parisa. I am the smartest of the bunch, and it's not even close.

And next Christmas, I'll hear about that comment.

RAT
TO: MY FAMILY

RULES FOR THIS YEAR'S CHRISTMAS VISIT:

NO JUDGING ME. THAT INCLUDES MY CLOTHES, WEIGHT, CAR, AND WHO I'M DATING.

NO DISCUSSING POLITICS. YOU ARE ALL LOONS.

I do not find your baby/small child as endearing as you do. Please keep this in mind when they are screaming or throwing objects at my head.

Please don't tell me how to live my life. Remember, I see you as loons.

12/13

And please do not brag about your own life. It makes me want to shove your head into the rear end of the turkey.

Lastly, none of these rules apply to me. I AM GREAT.

COMMUNICATION IS THE KEY TO A HAPPY FAMILY.

This was a popular strip. Apparently, many people have loons in their family.

Someone (maybe me) was feeling like his son (maybe Thomas) was not answering his texts when he went off to college. Oooh, snap. Take that, Thomas.

True Stephan Fact: I do this all the time. But I not only knock on wood, I knock three times with both hands in unison. And if someone else says something promising about my life, I make *them* knock three times with both hands. It's rather out of control.

I truly cannot conceive of why people do this. For me, you can put it up there with all of life's great mysteries, like the Kennedy assassination and the appeal of walnuts.

Thank you for downloading our new smartphone app.

TERMS AND CONDITIONS
Click to [READ]
Click to [ACCEPT]

[READ]
CLICK

Wow, okay. You're the first guy who didn't just click ACCEPT. But okay, here goes.

TERMS AND CONDITIONS

You have no rights.

We will violate your privacy.

We will track your every movement.

We will sell all of this information to anyone who wants it.

12/20

If we find anything really embarrassing, we will pass it around the office and laugh.

All of the above may accidentally be exposed to the entire world.

If so, oopsy-doopsies.

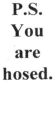

P.S. You are hosed.

NEVER READ THE TERMS AND CONDITIONS.

This was another popular strip. What is the point of agreeing to "terms and conditions" if not one single user ever reads them? Those terms could say anything. You can be agreeing to letting an elephant trample your nuts. Walnuts, of course.

I'm often asked what my relatives think of the strip. The most common response I hear from them is "I read it, but I don't usually understand it."

Join the crowd.

Here's how solely responsible my wife is for our annual Christmas card. People email me and say, "Great Christmas card." And I say, "Really? What was on it?"

This strip wasted gallons and gallons of newspaper ink. Good thing I don't have to pay for that.

This strip makes me laugh. Rat is definitely my favorite character.

This strip ran on Christmas Day and yet has nothing to do with Christmas. Unless you consider a fat smoker with a man on his back Christmassy.

Hey look, another Christmassy strip. A hamster avoiding Ebola.

When I was a kid, I used to write a one-page newsletter called the *Pastis Family Gazette* that I would put on the refrigerator. It contained scandalous stories about each family member. I found it very compelling.

The reaction to this surprised me. On the one hand, it was very popular, as many people apparently feel the same way about top knots. On the other hand, it triggered these strange, passionate complaints, like this one:

I would be violently angry and upset if someone decided arbitrarily to cut my usual hairstyle. . . . Perhaps consider not posting/printing such irrelevant, hateful, violent comic strips in future.

Bonus Fun Fact: I have a gray Honda Accord. And it can go 160 miles per hour.

YOU KNOW THAT CUTE FAMILY PORTRAIT SOME PEOPLE TAKE NOWADAYS WHERE EACH OF THEM DRESSES UP IN MATCHING CLOTHES?

YEAH, WHY?

IT MAKES ME SICK.

I HATE WHEN I AGREE WITH YOU.

CONGRESS, DO SOMETHING!

And it's always white shirts and blue jeans. Something's wrong with those people.

HEY, PIG... ANY NEW YEAR'S RESOLUTIONS THIS YEAR?

JUST THIS NEW 'EAT WHAT YOU WANT' DIET.

HOW DOES IT WORK?

YOU GET FAT.

SOUNDS LIKE YOU DON'T KNOW A LOT ABOUT NUTRITION.

WHAT CAN I GET YOU TO DRINK?

DO YOU HAVE WARM BEAVERS GETTING OLDER?

WHAT'S THAT?

I DUNNO. BUT RIGHT HERE YOU OFFER A WARM BEAVER THAT AGES.

'WARM BEVERAGES.'

THAT DOESN'T SOUND NEARLY AS INTERESTING.

"Warm beaver" is dangerously close to being dangerously inappropriate. I will say no more.

New Hampshire's state motto is the drama queen of state mottos.

Goat is reading a great book called *Destiny of the Republic*, in which the author explains how President Garfield would have survived the bullet wound he received, but for the doctors who stuck their finger inside it to try and get the bullet out. He died from the infection they caused.

When I was a young kid in the 1970s, my family would go on vacation to Balboa Island, California. My parents would give me enough money to take a ferry to an arcade and spend hours in the arcade by myself. Then I would come back when it got dark. Times have changed.

And dat when mom ees grow tiny leetle paws, like hamster paws.

REALLY?

Reely. So small dey call dem 'mini' paws. And dat how it get its name.

THAT IS NOT WHAT MENOPAUSE IS.

HELP.

Tomorrow me teach you 'bout hot flushes.

I'm fairly certain my comic strip causes a lot of uncomfortable conversations between kids and their parents. No need to thank me.

I THINK I JUST DID THE BEST WRITING OF MY LIFE.

GOOD FOR YOU, GOAT. POST IT ON THE INTERNET FOR ALL THE NICE PEOPLE TO SEE.

GOOD IDEA.

＊CLICK＊

MEH Embarrassing TRY MUCH?
#%&#$ you, poser. YOU %#&
DON'T QUIT SUCK, @$#
YOUR DAY BRO $#%
JOB!!!!!!!!! What crap.

I'VE MET NICER PEOPLE IN A PRISON RIOT.

OH, YEAH. PRISON'S MUCH FRIENDLIER.

When you first start doing anything creative, you are constantly checking the internet to see what people are saying about your work. But at some point into your career, you stop, because you realize that the range of discussion is always the same.

I'VE DETERMINED THAT THE INTERNET IS BESIEGED BY PEOPLE WHO JUST WANT TO VENT ANONYMOUSLY.

SO?

SO TO MAKE THE INTERNET A KINDER PLACE, I'VE DECIDED TO GIVE THOSE PEOPLE AN ALTERNATIVE VENUE.

'MAD MEN' SUCKS AFTER SEASON FIVE!!

The BOX O' ANONY-MOUS VENTING

NOT AS SATISFYING.

SHOUT LOUDER.

The biggest failure of a comic strip is when people simply don't get it. And I knew a fair number of people would get stuck on the term "incontinent." Thus, Rat's tagline in the last panel.

"Pre-owned" is really a great term. It eliminates all of the pejorative connotation that comes with the word "used."

If you're keeping score at home, two of these last three *Pearls* strips contain poop jokes. I take pride in that.

For me, if this occurs during a Warriors game, it really is an emergency. I turn the room upside down and hyperventilate. If necessary, I cry.

I now buy underwear with no labels. And if that's not inside information, I don't know what is.

If asked to choose between a life filled with love and one filled
with cheese, I would be hard-pressed to decide.

Note that Rat is reading the *Post-Dispatch*, a St. Louis, Missouri, newspaper. It's hidden gems like that which make me the brilliant creator that I am.

Strange but True Stephan Fact: On a recent trip to India (18-hour flight), a woman asked if I would switch seats to give her teenage daughter a chance to see the takeoff and landing (mine was a window seat). I felt bad, so I said yes. When I got to my new seat, I realized I was surrounded by mothers and their babies. The babies cried throughout the trip, and it was the worst flight of my life.

Staci really did this! So I am now an unwilling organ donor.

When I was a little kid, eating watermelon meant constantly checking for these big black seeds that you had to either spit out or choke on. Then, at some point in my adulthood, watermelons no longer had those big black seeds. That, in my opinion, is the most important event of the last 30 years.

Happens every single time I buy a computer or phone.

Danny Donkey's girlfriend was angry.

So she gave him an ultimatum.

"Here," she said, handing him an envelope. "Write down your passion and slip it in here, and in six weeks we'll open the envelope and see if you've taken any concrete steps towards achieving your passion."

So Danny Donkey did what she asked.

But then did nothing.

When the six weeks were up, Danny's girlfriend confronted him.

OH, DANNY... YOU DID NOTHING TO PURSUE YOUR PASSION... THAT'S SO AWFUL... WHAT WAS IT, ANYWAYS?

1/24

Sit on the couch and drink beer.

Danny's girlfriend left him anyways.

BUT HE PURSUED HIS PASSION!

LIFE JUST ISN'T FAIR.

BEING LAZY IS NOT A PASSION!

My passion was to find a job where I could sit in my underwear all day at home. And I achieved it. God bless America.

I would tell more dentist jokes if I didn't have to draw that stupid chair every time.

I floss twice a year. The day before each of my two appointments. Kids, don't try this at home.

HEY, GOAT, I'D LIKE YOU TO MEET JIM, 'THE GUY WHO MAKES BAD LIFE CHOICES.'

I'D TALK MORE, BUT I HAVE TO CHEAT ON MY WIFE WITH HER SISTER AND RIP OFF A BIKER GANG IN A METHAMPHETAMINE DEAL.

HE'LL BE A SHORT TERM CHARACTER.

It may seem odd, but this strip shows how much the comics page has changed in the past few years. When *Pearls* first started, I was not allowed to mention drugs, certainly not something as serious as methamphetamine. And now I can. Perhaps I've just burned out all of the newspaper editors, who cried and went home.

WHERE WERE YOU TODAY, RAT?

SHOPPING. I GOT A LAZY SUSAN TO PUT ON OUR KITCHEN TABLE.

I'M NOT DOING A G#$%#*$ THING.

SUSAN HAS A VERY BAD ATTITUDE.

HEY, RAT. WELCOME TO MY COCKTAIL PARTY. CAN I GET YOU A BEVERAGE?

DUDE... TALK LIKE A NORMAL PERSON.

WHAT DO YOU MEAN?

YOU DON'T HAVE TO SAY 'BEVERAGE.' JUST SAY 'DRINK' AND STOP BEING A HOITY TOITY FATFACE.

CAN I GET YOU A LIBATION?

CURSE YOUR SNOOTY FATFACE!

I really cannot stand the word "beverage." Particularly when it is preceded by the words "refreshing" or "tasty."

1/31

A Story from Prehistoric Times: When I was in college in 1989, I was supposed to meet a friend in Italy. She did not show up. Because there were no such things as cell phones or the internet, I had to get a whole bunch of change, go to a pay phone, and call my mom in the United States. She proceeded to call the girl's mom (also in the United States) and asked her that if her daughter called home, to please tell her that I would meet her at a certain location at a certain time. A lot has changed.

77

It is here that I must admit the following: I actually like tofu.

My subtle prediction that 2016 was going to be a bad year.

Am I the only person who ate animal crackers by first biting off all the heads? Surely not.

The best thing about comic strips is how subversive they can be. You can sneak in little thoughts that really can't appear in other parts of the newspaper.

This strip may have been the single most disaster-laden (that is, cursed) strip I have ever done. Let me count the ways:

1) It is based on a Bruce Springsteen song lyric ("Wendy, let me in, I want to be your friend, I want to guard your dreams and visions"). I changed it to "Wendy's, let me in, I want to be your Fred, I want to guard your reams and fissions." EXCEPT, I messed up and forgot to change "friend" to "Fred" in the edition that ran in newspapers (it's been corrected here in the book). So, really, in the newspaper, the first line of the pun was no pun at all. It just said "Wendy's, let me in, I want to be your friend," which is pretty much just the song lyric.

2) As if that wasn't confusing enough, a lot of people did not know the song lyric. I thought everyone knew the words to "Born to Run." I was not correct. This led to a lot of feedback that looked like this:

"Now you've done it. You printed a pun that I don't get. First time EVER. You owe me, a faithful putter-upper with you, an explanation, and if it's obscure enough, an apology."

3) But this strip wasn't done being cursed. Because in many of the newspapers where *Pearls* ran that day, someone at the syndicate accidentally deleted my strip and replaced it with a strip called *Off the Mark*. So many Sunday newspaper readers didn't even see *Pearls* that day. And, of course, one of those newspapers where it was deleted was the *Newark Star-Ledger*, the biggest newspaper in the state of New Jersey, Bruce Springsteen's home. So, a disaster from start to finish.

80

Kids, this is true. Feel free to cut this out and show it to your algebra teacher.

Tardigrades! They have survived all of the cataclysmic events that have otherwise destroyed most life on this earth. You have to admire their spirit.

I wasn't sure I could say "anal-retentive" on the comics page. Turns out you can.

I like to run these strips near Valentine's Day, when cynicism is at an all-time high.

A venereal disease joke, three days after using the phrase "anal-retentive." It's a wonder I remain on the comics page.

This may have been the most popular strip of the year. I like the double meaning of Pig's line in the last panel.

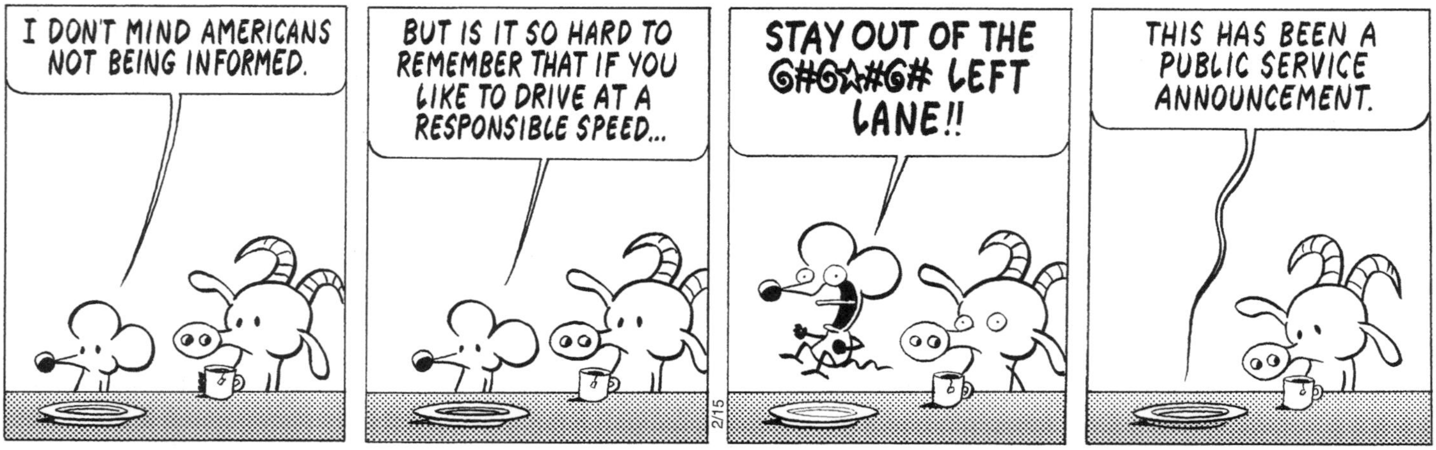
I DON'T MIND AMERICANS NOT BEING INFORMED.
BUT IS IT SO HARD TO REMEMBER THAT IF YOU LIKE TO DRIVE AT A RESPONSIBLE SPEED...
STAY OUT OF THE @#@☆#@# LEFT LANE!!
THIS HAS BEEN A PUBLIC SERVICE ANNOUNCEMENT.
2/15

And because *Pearls* is read internationally, let me further the public announcement for those of you slow drivers in Britain, Australia, India, and elsewhere:

Stay out of the #@$#*@# right lane!

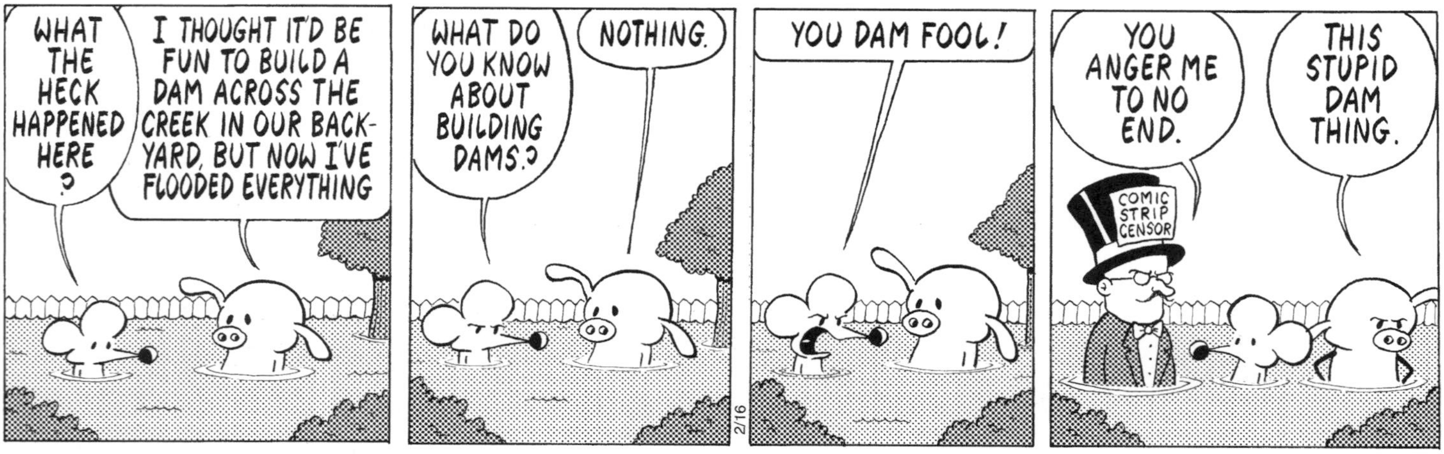
WHAT THE HECK HAPPENED HERE?
I THOUGHT IT'D BE FUN TO BUILD A DAM ACROSS THE CREEK IN OUR BACK-YARD, BUT NOW I'VE FLOODED EVERYTHING
WHAT DO YOU KNOW ABOUT BUILDING DAMS?
NOTHING.
YOU DAM FOOL!
2/16
YOU ANGER ME TO NO END.
COMIC STRIP CENSOR
THIS STUPID DAM THING.

And now I'm using the word "damn." Well, sort of. This was a banner month for the groundbreaking pioneer that is me.

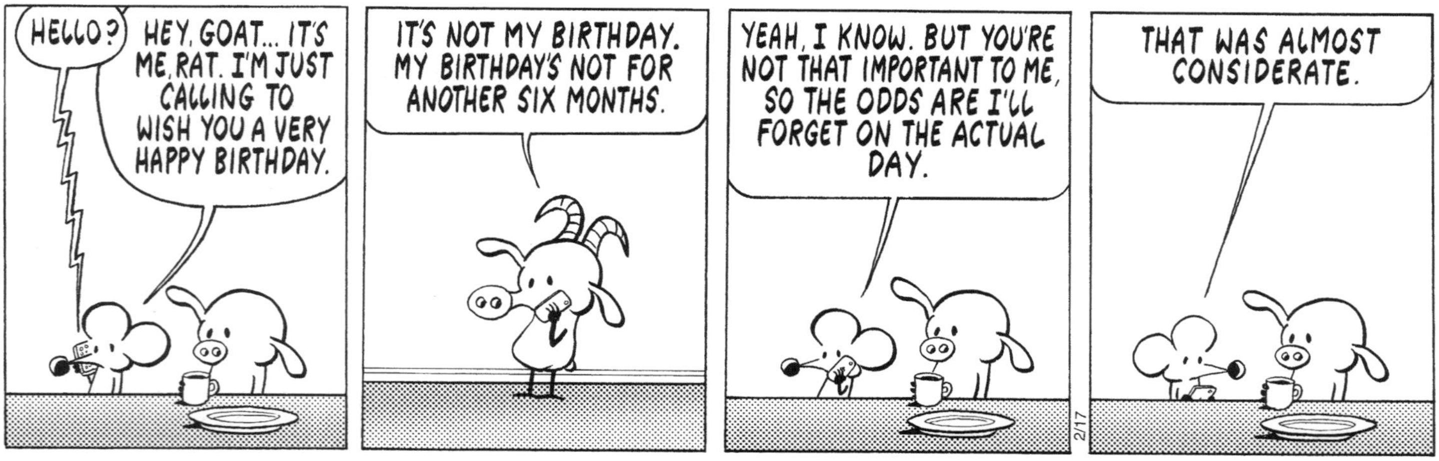
HELLO?
HEY, GOAT... IT'S ME, RAT. I'M JUST CALLING TO WISH YOU A VERY HAPPY BIRTHDAY.
IT'S NOT MY BIRTHDAY. MY BIRTHDAY'S NOT FOR ANOTHER SIX MONTHS.
YEAH, I KNOW. BUT YOU'RE NOT THAT IMPORTANT TO ME, SO THE ODDS ARE I'LL FORGET ON THE ACTUAL DAY.
2/17
THAT WAS ALMOST CONSIDERATE.

Little-Known Fun Fact: There are some people from a large female scouting organization that shall not be named who do not take kindly to strips such as this.

This is taken from our own lives. We have deer that live in our yard and they eat just about everything. Though they have not yet raided our refrigerator.

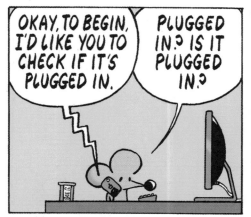

2/21

Judging by how often tech support asks if your computer is plugged in,
I'm guessing a lot of people make this mistake.

This marked the introduction of the bad grandparents. It just made me laugh to think of grandparents who didn't want anything to do with their grandchildren.

"Hell" is another word that can cause issues with some readers.

Another venereal disease joke. My, February was "Educate the Youngsters" month.

I'm surprised no one has done this joke before. It seems so obvious.

I wonder how much newspaper ink it took to print the last two panels of this strip in 800 or so newspapers. I'm guessing more than I could drink.

Educational Fact Time: What Goat says in the third panel is true. But, in fact, what occurs is that the candidates and the super PACs *do* coordinate, which is why very rich people can now control political candidates.

I'm writing this commentary at the end of 2017. And I think a lot of people would share Pig's sentiment for the year that just passed.

This was also one of the year's most popular strips. The image from the third panel even got turned into a T-shirt.

90

Goodness. I get away with murder.

So you can't call someone an "ass" on the comics page. But "ass" is a perfectly acceptable synonym for a donkey. So I brought in a smart donkey character and named him "Wise Ass."

91

I present this clarification from a volunteer for a large female scouting organization that shall remain nameless:

The sale of Girl Scout cookies is a BUSINESS run by girls and their adult volunteer helpers. It is part of the educational programming of Girl Scouts, which aims to help young ladies learn about economics, salesmanship and marketing, public speaking, and goal setting.

So, apparently, they do not actually use the money to buy grenades.

LOOK, GOAT, I GOT NEW LOUVER SHUTTERS.

WHAT'S THAT FUNNY THING STICKING OUT OF THEM?

THAT'S THE LIVER-SHAPED CRANK THAT OPENS THEM. MAKES FOR AN EASY GRIP. DO YOU LIKE IT?

I LOVE IT.

SO YOU'RE A LIVER LEVER LOUVER LOVER?

NOBODY LOVES YOU.

Rat raises a valid point.

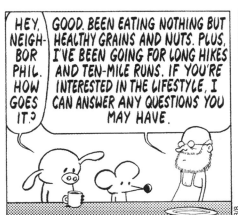

HEY, NEIGHBOR PHIL. HOW GOES IT?

GOOD. BEEN EATING NOTHING BUT HEALTHY GRAINS AND NUTS. PLUS, I'VE BEEN GOING FOR LONG HIKES AND TEN-MILE RUNS. IF YOU'RE INTERESTED IN THE LIFESTYLE, I CAN ANSWER ANY QUESTIONS YOU MAY HAVE.

I HAVE A QUESTION.

YES, RAT?

WHY DO HEALTH-CONSCIOUS PEOPLE LOOK THE LEAST HEALTHY?

HE TOOK HIS GRANOLA AND WENT HOME.

AT LEAST BEER GIVES ME A ROSY GLOW!!

HI MOM. HI DAD. WHERE ARE MY KIDS?

THEY WENT FOR A BIKE RIDE.

WHO'S WATCHING THEM?

WATCHING THEM? WELL, NOT US. WE'RE READING THE PAPER.

AAHHHHH

PARENTING IS DIFFERENT NOW.

My parents had no idea where I went on my bike rides. Or if I was even on a bike ride. As long as I showed up for dinner, they correctly assumed I hadn't died.

So this one is straight out of my own life as well. Way back in 1980, when I was 12, my parents let me fly by myself to Pittsburgh. As far as I can remember, I did not wander into any steel-factory cauldrons and die.

I like making Rat as far right politically as possible. Though it's getting harder and harder to compete with reality these days.

I think Pig's line about the "CEO consumption fee" is the best part of this strip.

Panel 1:
WHAT ARE ALL THESE LOCKS ON THIS BRIDGE, GOAT?

THEY'RE LOVE LOCKS. COUPLES PUT THEM THERE AS A SYMBOL OF THEIR EVERLASTING, UNBREAKABLE LOVE.

Panel 3:
THERE WERE RELATIONSHIP ISSUES.

I got this idea from a bridge I saw when I was in Finland. It was just covered with these locks. Apparently, they can be a real problem, because they add a tremendous amount of weight to the structure, causing portions of it to collapse. This proves that any romantic relationship ultimately weighs you down and destroys you.

Panel 1:
WANT TO BUY SOME COOKIES, SIR?

SURE, L'IL SCOUTS. WHAT ARE YOU RAISING MONEY FOR?

SALE

Panel 2:
TO FIGHT THE DRUG WAR.

GOOD FOR YOU. HOW ARE YOU GONNA DO THAT?

COOKIE SALE

Panel 3:
BY PROTECTING OUR TURF AGAINST THE OTHER CARTELS.

COOKIE SALE

Panel 4:
I LIKE TO REWARD AMBITION.

Now the scouts are selling drugs. I'm out of control.

Panel 1:
HI MOM. HI DAD. I JUST CAME BY TO SAY I WON'T BE BRINGING JIMMY OVER TODAY. I HAVE TO TAKE HIM TO HIS SOCCER GAME.

DIDN'T YOU GO TO HIS LAST SOCCER GAME?

Panel 2:
YEAH. I GO TO ALL OF HIS GAMES. I HAVEN'T MISSED ONE IN FOUR YEARS.

Panel 3:
HAHAHAHAH

Panel 4:
I'M SERIOUS.

YOU MIGHT BE OBSESSIVE.

GET A HOBBY, SWEETIE.

Another one out of my own life. I attended most of my daughter's basketball games. But I can't remember my parents coming to any of mine. Maybe they thought I was still in Pittsburgh.

L'il Scouts selling drugs. Chickens being killed. What else will happen this week?

So this one triggered a rather bizarre complaint about the fact that I was making light of the abuse of children, which I thought was ridiculous. I often think the strip is just a lightning rod for anger that people have on given subjects. They're not really that mad at me specifically. They just need a place to put their rage.

I don't do the croc strips as often as I used to. Some people think that's a good thing.
Others say they miss them. It's always hard to find the right balance.

I went to India not too long ago and got to go to both Mumbai and Goa (though not to New Delhi). It was one of the best trips I've ever taken. I was surprised at how many *Pearls* fans there were there.

Wow. Did I get away with that one, too? I need a chaperone.

I sometimes wonder why any character ever sits next to Rat in the diner. Don't they read this strip?

Elly Elephant is named for my niece Elenique. Who as far as I know has never dated a hippo. Or anyone else outside of her species.

This was based on an incident where students from my beloved alma mater, the University of California at Berkeley, tried to bar comedian Bill Maher (the host of HBO's *Real Time*) from speaking.

Having Rat run for president in the insane political year that was 2016 allowed me to comment on a lot of what was going on in the country.

This was an easy joke. But it made me laugh.

Although it has not yet caught me sunbathing in the nude, I understand that the Google Street View truck has indeed caught many strange things, from a man stuffed in a trunk to a guy robbing a house.

I have more Twitter followers than Johnson.

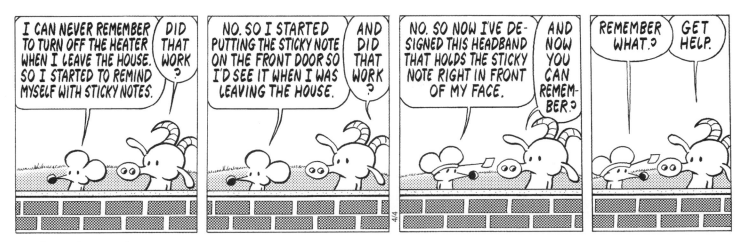

My front door at this very moment:

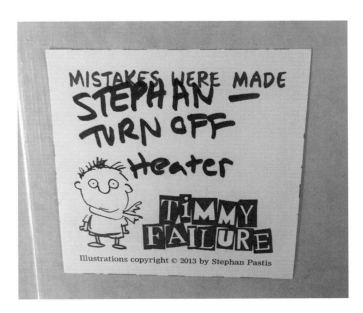

I think the look on Bob's face as he floats away is pretty perfect.

This is totally my trick.

If you're keeping track at home, I've now mocked vegans, cyclists, and triathletes. Basically, all the healthy people.

'THERE ARE SO MANY WAYS TO DIE IN THIS WORLD,' THOUGHT ANGRY BOB. 'AND I DO NOT WANT TO DIE.'

SO ANGRY BOB ATTENDED A SAFETY SEMINAR AT HIS LOCAL FIRE DEPARTMENT AND LEARNED ABOUT VARIOUS FIRE DANGERS. LIKE NOT CLEANING YOUR DRYER'S LINT SCREEN.

AND SO BOB WENT HOME AND DUTIFULLY CLEANED HIS LINT SCREEN.

AND WENT TO SLEEP HAPPY.

ZZZZZZZ

AND THAT NIGHT, THE DISCARDED LINT RE-FORMED ITSELF INTO LINTZILLA.

AND SUFFOCATED BOB IN HIS SLEEP.

'SO NEVER CLEAN YOUR LINT SCREEN.'

DO NOT TELL PEOPLE THAT.

THERE ARE SO MANY WAYS TO *DIE!*

I think Lintzilla should be a new character.

See, I could have said "ass" here if the man had been walking around with a donkey.

Another popular strip. There was so much anxiety in this election year that it was pretty easy to tap into it.

Hey, a Bruce Springsteen strip that didn't get all screwed up. That's progress.

Alas, no actual censorship. Here's a look at the original strip before I added all the little black rectangles in Photoshop.

I STARTED A NEW BUSINESS.

DOING WHAT?

I SELL PEOPLE THEIR OWN CANNING MACHINE AND A SUPPLY OF FRUIT PICKED IN THE AFRICAN SAVANNA.

WHAT KIND OF FRUIT?

MOSTLY BANANAS, WHICH THEY THEN CAN THEMSELVES.

AND WHAT DO THEY DO WITH THEM?

SELL THEM IN COVERED LITTLE POOLSIDE HUTS, BUT SOME CITIES WANT TO BAN THE STRUCTURE.

WHY?

I DUNNO. BUT TO HELP MY CHANCES, I GOT A CELEBRITY PARTNER TO PUT HER NAME ON THE BUSINESS. IT'S THAT WOMAN WHO TURNS THE LETTERS ON 'WHEEL OF FORTUNE.' NOW MAYBE THE CITIES WON'T DO WHAT THEY'RE THREATENING TO DO.

4/17

WHAT ARE CITIES THREATENING TO DO?

BAN A 'VANNA CAN A SAVANNA BANANA' CABANA.

AND JUST LIKE THAT, ANOTHER SUNDAY IS RUINED.

I referenced *Wheel of Fortune* in a strip a few years prior, and the show gave me this signed photo:

I liked this one. It was an easy pun and the words sound exactly alike.

When I travel, I love to see sites that were significant in the life of Martin Luther King, Jr. So far, I've seen where he was born, his father's church in Atlanta, his own church and office in Montgomery, the place where he gave the "mountaintop" speech, and the motel where he was killed.

WHAT ARE YOU LISTENING TO, STEPH?

THIS GREAT STATION PLAYS ALL THE MUSIC I ALWAYS LOVED IN COLLEGE AND STUFF, LIKE 'GUNS N' ROSES' AND 'NIRVANA.'

OH, YEAH, THAT'S THE 'GOLDEN OLDIES' STATION.

AND THEN HE CRIED AND LEFT.

WHAT'S THE MATTER WITH YOU?

I HAVE TO GO TO A DINNER PARTY WITH A BUNCH OF ACADEMIC TYPES, AND I'M AFRAID I'M GONNA LOOK STUPID.

JUST TALK LIKE THEY DO AND USE ALL THE BUZZWORDS. YOU KNOW, LIKE 'EXISTENTIAL ANGST,' AND 'PARADIGM SHIFT.'

AND THANKS FOR LETTING ME USE YOUR BATHROOM, WHERE I RELIEVED MY EXISTENTIAL ANGST WITH A NICE PARADIGM SHIFT.

This is a rare strip in that the punch line in the final panel has 19 words. I usually like it to be six or less, maybe ten at the most. Shorter is generally better.

HEY, STEPH, THIS IS JOHN GLYNN, THE HEAD OF YOUR SYNDICATE, AND I HAVE SOME REAL FAMILY-FRIENDLY, CHUCKLE-FILLED IDEAS FOR YOUR COMIC.

OH. OKAY. WHAT ARE THEY?

OKAY, WELL, IN THIS FIRST STRIP, THE—

SPLOOSH

FLUSH

IS IT RAINING THERE?

John Glynn really is the head of my syndicate. And his head really is that big.

Every Sunday I eat breakfast with my family. And my daughter, Julia, always reads *Slylock Fox* and does all the puzzles, particularly the one where you have to find the six differences between the panels. So to get her attention (and get her to read *my* strip), I disguised it as *Slylock* and even snuck her name into it. Kudos to you if you can find her name.

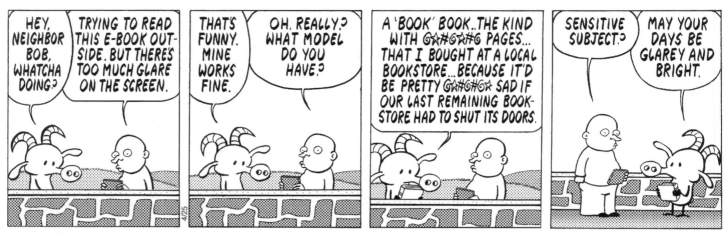

This really is true. We all need to support our local bookstores.

Over the past several years, I've made a fair number of trips to England, and the differences between our common language always amuse me. My favorite is what they call the trunk of the car: the boot. And what they call the hood: the bonnet.

Point of Clarification: I do not write my initials on my underwear. I stopped doing that years ago, when I was 44.

As I travel more, I notice that rooftop bars are quite the trend. From Nashville to Charleston to Portland, there are great ones everywhere.

Whenever I want people to look particularly dumb, I give them those puffy lips.

My key to flying is to always take a window seat (where I can sleep with my head against the side of the plane) and pick red-eye flights whenever I can. Then I fall right asleep and wake up just as we land.

A representative of a very large female scouting organization would like you to know that they do not kill people. And if they did, they wouldn't give a merit badge for it.

HEY, LIQUOR STORE LARRY... HOW'S BUSINESS?

GOOD. MY STORE'S NOW BIG ENOUGH THAT THE DISTRIBUTOR GIVES ME MORE LIQUOR THAN I ORDER. AND THE OVERAGE IS FREE.

BECAUSE HE DOESN'T WANT TO LOSE BUSINESS?

YEP. HE DOES IT FOR THE BIG STORES.

THAT'S EXTRAORDINARY.

NOT REALLY. I HAVE AVERAGE OVERAGE BEVERAGE LEVERAGE.

ARE YOU DRINKING AS YOU WRITE THESE?

I am not.

Dear Mr. Congressman, I know that now you only represent rich people who give you lots of money.

But I don't have any money.

So here's a crushed donut.

WE'LL SEE HOW MUCH PULL THAT GIVES ME.

HEY, NEIGHBOR BOB. WHAT ARE YOU DOING?

I'M TIRED OF PEOPLE CRITICIZING ME FOR BEING DEPRESSED, SO I FORMED THIS GROUP. I'M NOW A 'DARN OKAY PERSON THAT IS DEPRESSED.'

DOES IT RUN IN THE FAMILY?

YEP. MY DAUGHTER HAS IT ALSO. SO SHE'S ONE, TOO.

I'M WHAT, DAD?

YOU'RE A 'D.O.P.T.I.D.'

SHE TOOK IT WORSE THAN I THOUGHT.

She may be adopted, but they have the same nose.

True Fact: The man who invented the Pringles can was buried in a Pringles can.

To paraphrase an old commercial: This is your bird. This is your bird on drugs.

On the day this ran, I posted it on Twitter and received a nice thank-you from George Carlin's daughter. But the next day, the Harrisburg *Patriot-News* ran this letter about *Pearls*:

> **I'm writing politely and sincerely to ask the *Patriot-News* to please find a more decent wholesome and innocently humorous comic strip as soon as possible, to replace that travesty called *Pearls Before Swine*.**
>
> **Every week I read it and I keep hoping the content gets better, but most of the time, I end up very disappointed, to say the least. The humor is often plain sick, sometimes downright disgusting**

Maybe the national holiday for George Carlin was more than he could take.

I'm hoping that at least one pilot out there has this strip taped somewhere inside the cockpit.

This just makes me laugh.

5/15

For those who might not know, I actually wrote an animated *Peanuts* special. It's called *Happiness Is a Warm Blanket, Charlie Brown.*

This is taken from what Kobe Bryant said when he retired from the NBA. He just said "Mamba out" and put down the microphone.

This was a fun experiment to see if I could get a photo into the strip. It took a bit of technical help from the people at the syndicate, but ultimately it worked pretty well. Naturally, I wore my Cal hat.

I've been out on that porch for a very long time.

The council of aliens met at alien headquarters.

We are an advanced race, but that poor race of humans is not. They are sad, silly, and stupid.

So the council of aliens passed a resolution.

We will save the human race from itself.

And so, using all of their advanced technology, the aliens constructed their gift to humanity.

And fired it in a rocket to earth.

And thus, I was born.

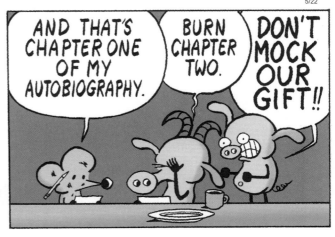

AND THAT'S CHAPTER ONE OF MY AUTOBIOGRAPHY.

BURN CHAPTER TWO.

DON'T MOCK OUR GIFT!!

A fellow syndicated cartoonist (whom I will not name) once told me that he thought he might have been put here by aliens. That inspired this.

In the entire 16 years of *Pearls*, this is the first time we have ever accidentally repeated a strip. It ran on February 11 as well. I still don't know quite how it happened. But because he's not here to defend himself, I'm gonna blame syndicate president John Glynn. He's the one with the large head.

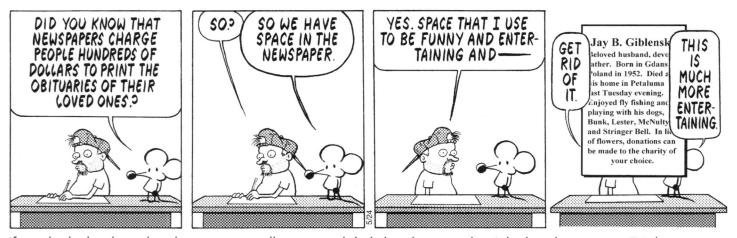

If you look closely at the obituary, you will see my subtle little tribute to what I think is the greatest TV show ever written, *The Wire*. Bunk, Lester, McNulty, and Stringer Bell were all characters in the show.

WHATCHA READING, GOAT?

A BOOK ABOUT THE DIFFERENT PARTS OF THE BRAIN. YOU KNOW, LIKE THE CEREBRAL CORTEX, THE FRONTAL LOBE, THE HIPPOCAMPUS.

SORRY, PIG...DO YOU KNOW WHAT ALL THAT IS?

THE HIPPOCAMPUS IS WHERE THE HIPPOS GO TO COLLEGE.

NO.

THEY MUST HAVE VERY LARGE CHAIRS.

I like to read books on the mysteries of the human brain. And when I do, the subject generally finds its way into the strip.

HEY, JEF THE CYCLIST. I HEAR THE CITY IS PUTTING BIKE LANES ON EVERY STREET. ISN'T THAT GREAT?

NOT GREAT ENOUGH.

WHAT ELSE DO YOU WANT?

FOR PEOPLE TO CLEAR A SIX-FOOT-WIDE PATH WHEN ANY OF US CYCLISTS IS WALKING AROUND, SO THAT WE DON'T GET YOUR ORDINARINESS ON US.

I FEEL LIKE I'M SITTING TOO CLOSE.

YOU ARE. CLEAR THE JEF PATH.

I WANT MORE OF EVERYTHING. AND I WANT IT BIGGER AND FASTER.

BUT WHERE DOES THAT ALL END?

WHEN I'VE GOT THE MOSTEST OF THE BIGGEST AND THE FASTEST.

SO GRAMMAR'S A HIGH PRIORITY?

I WANT THE BESTEST.

Speaking of grammar, I recently had a woman write me about my use of the word "anyways." She said:

I often laugh out loud at some of your strips and share them with my friends and family. However, today you used the word "anyways" which I did not laugh about. The correct word is "ANYWAY."

So I wrote back:

**Wow, that's embarrassing. I did not know that.
Anyways, thanks for reading the strip.**

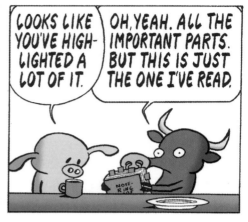

I kind of blew this one. First off, I should have run it around Christmas. Second, the emphasis is on the wrong syllables. In other words, you sing the song line like this: "RuDOLPH the RED-nosed REINdeer." But the way the pun reads, the emphasis is on the wrong words, that is, "RUDE off the read NOSE ring, DARE." The pun has to at least match the rhythm of the original line or it doesn't work.

I thought I would get a little more flak from this, given that I'm sort of mocking a character from the Bible. But if there were complaints, I didn't hear about them.

And this is the strip that I surely thought would get me in trouble. First off, it's a character from the Bible. Second, he's partying with a hot woman. Third, and most important, the line "party on the poop deck" can be taken a number of different ways, none of which are wholesome.

No gaffers complained. Though if they did, I wouldn't know what a gaffer looked like.

I'm going to go out on a limb and say this is the first time anyone has ever been shown on the comics page (bird or otherwise) using a bidet. No need to applaud.

These Abbott and Costello strips are by far the hardest to write because they involve two separate conversations, and each line has to work in both conversations.

133

Rat's statement in the first panel is true.

I do this all the time. Someone says they will meet me somewhere at 7:15, and I reply, "Can we make it 7:16?" They never know what to say.

I think when I looked up what a gaffer was, I found all these other film industry titles, resulting in this strip and the next.

Okay, that's supposed to be Dolly Parton. And the strip doesn't work if you don't know that. So I'm telling you. Too bad I can't print these comments in the actual newspaper.

6/12

All true. And all learned the hard way.

I never pick up the house phone. It can only be a telemarketer. Everyone else uses my cell phone.

During my tour of the Pentagon, nobody offered me a drone. That's unfortunate.

I saw my first drone while walking in downtown Los Angeles. I think it was just filming something. At least I hope so.

I was a huge baseball card collector as a little kid. The 1909 Honus Wagner card is the most valuable card ever. It recently sold for $3 million.

6/19

I really like this strip. Now that's not particularly insightful, but they can't all be winners.

I sort of got this idea from a funeral procession I watched in the French Quarter of New Orleans. As they marched, the friends of the deceased carried the barstool the man always sat on.

As a little kid growing up in the 1970s, I used to love *Battle of the Network Stars*. Actors from the competing networks (ABC, CBS, and NBC) used to compete against each other in various athletic events. I always rooted for ABC because that was the channel that had my favorite show, *Happy Days*.

Dumb friends: the key to feeling superior. At least that's my secret.

While I color the Sunday strips, I do not color the daily strips. I don't even see the color until the strip appears in newspapers. So I was really hoping the colorist would not give these two men dark-colored skin, thereby ruining the joke. As far as I know, that didn't happen. It's a bit of a risk to do the daily coloring like this, but so far, there have been very few errors.

THE SUNDAY PAPER IS TRADITION-ALLY KNOWN FOR ITS MANY COUP-ONS. BUT DO YOU REALLY NEED ANOTHER CHEAP HAM? SO TODAY WE OFFER YOU COUPONS YOU CAN REALLY USE.

ONE FREE PUNCH TO THE HEAD

to any non-blind person who wears their sunglasses indoors.

ONE FREE POP IN THE NOSE

to anyone who thinks I care about what kind of luxury sedan they just bought.

ONE FREE KICK TO THE OOMPA-LOOMPAS

of the next billionaire who asks my poor city to pay for his new stadium.

ONE FREE WAKE-UP CALL

to the Facebook friend who posts endless photos of themselves with their boyfriend or girlfriend on Valentine's Day, New Year's Eve, or at any other enjoyable event that I did not attend.

I do not like you.

AN EVEN BIGGER WAKE-UP CALL

to the Twitter friend who keeps posting their political opinion.

I muted you a long time ago.

ONE FREE BAT TO THE HAND

of any cartoonist who thinks it's clever or original to make himself a character in his own comic strip

The use of the word "oompa-loompas" as slang for male testicles is my greatest contribution to the English language.

Any similarity to a certain presidential candidate in 2016 is purely coincidental.

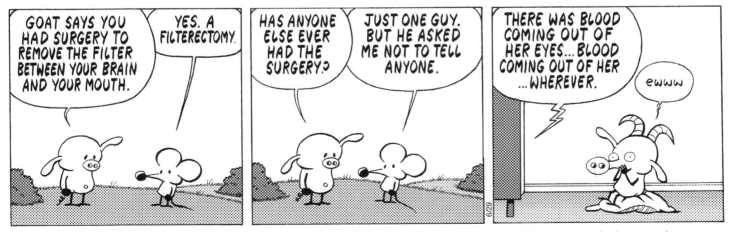

Okay, maybe not so coincidental. The quote in the last panel is something that Donald Trump said about TV host Megyn Kelly.

WHAT ARE YOU DOING, RAT?

ANALYZING ALL OF MY FAILED ROMANTIC RELATIONSHIPS TO DETERMINE IF THERE WERE ANY FACTORS COMMON TO EACH OF THEM.

HAVE YOU FOUND ANYTHING?

ME

HOW DO I BREAK UP WITH ME?

I am often asked at book signings who my favorite character is. Without question: Rat. I could write for him all day.

WHAT ARE YOU WATCHING, GOAT?

WIMBLEDON.

WHAT'S WIMBLEDON?

THIS TENNIS MATCH WHERE THE PLAYERS PLAY ON GRASS.

DRUG LEGALIZATION IS OUT OF CONTROL.

Most of the home appliances that the characters have (especially the TV) are out of the 1970s, as opposed to the present. That's not so much because it's when I grew up; it's more because those styles of TVs are a better visual shorthand for what a TV is supposed to look like (as opposed to a flat screen, which could just as easily be a computer monitor). Same for a phone with a long, curly cord.

HEY, PIG, HOW'S YOUR SATURDAY GOING?

GREAT. WE HAVE A HUGE LEAK IN OUR ROOF AND THE WATER IS JUST POURING IN.

WHY IS THAT GREAT?

I NO LONGER HAVE TO WATER OUR INDOOR PLANTS!

NOW THAT'S AN OPTIMIST.

7/3

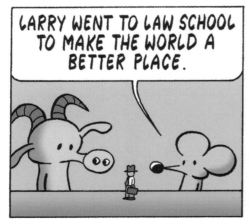

I was once Larry Lawyer. Though I didn't go to law school to make the world a better place. I just wanted money.

A reference to the 1960s band Cream. I'm sure I lost a few younger people on that one.

I've never had the urge to swim with dolphins. I fear they'd balance me on their noses, swim off, and hold me hostage.

Sadly, I think my piano teacher made me learn this song on the piano. Speaking of which, I hated taking piano lessons. My teacher used to come over to my house every Thursday for the lesson. I used to stand in the living room window hoping and praying that she wouldn't show up. About the only thing that would stop her was a really heavy rain (I don't think she liked driving in rain). So I always rooted for thunderstorms.

That is one strange-looking dog. Particularly in the third panel. I wish I could blame somebody else, but it appears I'm in charge here.

My daughter plays tennis for her high school team. One time when I went to watch her, there was a whole table of food outside the court. It was great. I ate chips, salad, and tons of Rice Krispies treats. Then my daughter told me the food was only for the players. And worse, the food I ate was the food brought by the *other* team. No wonder all those strange people were staring at me.

When I travel, I often come back with a lot of foreign currency. I figure it doesn't matter since I assume that one day I'll go back. So when I came back from a recent trip to India, I had a whole bunch of rupees, which I just held on to. But then the Indian government went and declared them invalid, allegedly as a way to crack down on counterfeiting. I think they were going after me specifically.

The numbers on the prisoners' uniforms are the birthdays of three of my cousins.

NONE OF MY TWEETS ARE GOING OUT TODAY.

YEAH. RAT WENT HUNTING.

SO?

HE SHOT THE TWITTER BIRD.

HE WAS MUCH TOO CHATTY.

One of the best things about Twitter and Facebook is that they give me the ability to connect with people I otherwise wouldn't know how to reach. For example, I recently posted on Facebook that I was going to Mexico City. A former congressional staffer saw the post and offered to set up a meeting between me and the U.S. ambassador to Mexico. I love stuff like that.

WHATCHA DOING, RAT?

I'M ON HOLD WITH AN AIRLINE AND A RECORDED VOICE IS APOLOGIZING FOR THE INCONVENIENCE AND TELLING ME THEY APPRECIATE MY BUSINESS.

WHICH IS NICE TO HEAR BUT BECOMES... SHEER G#%★#G# MOCKERY WHEN YOU'VE HEARD IT THIRTY-ONE @#★#G#% TIMES IN A ROW!!

MAYBE THEY REALLY REALLY APPRECIATE YOUR BUSINESS.

THEY SHOULD JUST SAY, 'YOU'RE SCREWED AND IT AMUSES US.'

This might have happened during a certain conversation between a cartoonist (maybe me) and an airline (maybe Southwest).

HEY, PIG... I HAVE SOMETHING TO TELL YOU, BUT PLEASE DON'T TAKE OFFENSE.

I WOULD NEVER DO THAT WITHOUT ASKING.

ASKING WHAT?

IF I COULD TAKE YOUR FENCE OR ANYONE ELSE'S.

LET'S START OVER.

LET'S. BECAUSE SO FAR, IT'S BEEN VERY OFFENSIVE.

7/17

Goat's statements in the first five panels of the strip are my current theory of life.
That said, I do not like sharing my peanuts.

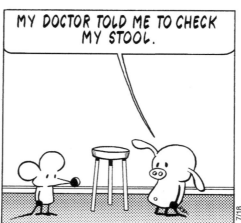

There used to be a drinking game when I was in college that revolved around the TV show *Cheers*. You had to drink every time a character said the word "drink" or "drank," and you had to drink when anyone said "Norm" (one of the character's names). There were other times you had to drink as well. In short, it was a very quick way to get blitzed.

This one is another indication of how much the comics page has changed. Before, whenever you mentioned a disorder (like ADD or ADHD), you were guaranteed to get complaints saying you were making fun of the condition. Nowadays, not nearly as much. Maybe all the complainers have ADD and can't focus long enough to write a complaint.

STEPHAN DOES A BOOK SIGNING

THANK YOU ALL FOR COMING TO THE BOOK SIGNING TONIGHT. MY EX-WIFE STACI IS ACTUALLY HERE IN THE FIRST ROW AND I'M THINKING MAYBE SHE'D LIKE TO BE INTRODUCED.

I'M THINKING NOT.

LOOK...SHE'S TELLING YOU YOU'RE NUMBER ONE.

I not so subtly used this strip to get in a plug for one of my recent collections, *I'm Only in This for Me.*

WHO'S YOUR SUPERHERO FRIEND?

'HOLD.'

HE'S GOT A SUPER GRIP?

HE CAN WAIT ON HOLD 'TIL HIS HEALTH INSURER ANSWERS.

THAT *IS* A SUPERPOWER.

I'LL OUTWAIT THEE, EVIL FOE!

CALL MINE NEXT.

My wife, Staci, makes all of these calls for me. She's *my* superhero.

WHAT'S PIG DOING?

HE GOT A JOB AS A QUEEN'S GUARD. HE'S NOT ALLOWED TO MOVE A MUSCLE.

CLICK *CLICK*

THERE GOES THAT JOB.

MIND HOLDING MY GUN WHILE I GO POTTY?

That last comment was uncharacteristically sweet. I promise not to do it again.

7/24

This was another popular strip.

I tried to make Pig's art look noticeably worse than mine. But it looks pretty much the same. I'm not sure what that says about my art.

IF YOU COULD HAVE A CONVERSATION WITH ONE PERSON, LIVING OR DEAD, WHO WOULD IT BE?

THE LIVING ONE.

YOU MUST THINK I'M REALLY STUPID.

This is the one and only time I ever intentionally repeated an old strip. That's because my syndicate was not keen on running the strip that I had scheduled that day. The strip that was *supposed* to run is right here:

HI, PIG. IT'S YOUR SISTER.

HI, SIS. WHAT'S GOING ON?

MY FRIEND AND ME ARE GOING TO THE MOVIES.

I THINK IT'S 'I', NOT 'ME'.

HUH?

I, SIS! I, SIS!

NATIONAL SECURITY AGENCY
Wiretap Division

NEVER CORRECT YOUR SISTER'S GRAMMAR.

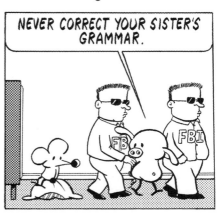

My editor at the syndicate was uncomfortable with the strip, given ISIS's prevalence in the news at the time and the horrific things they were doing (a lot of beheadings). I probably could have pushed it and at least argued for keeping it. But I agreed and told him to run a repeat.

HEY, GOAT. THIS IS MY PAL, LINDA. SHE'S NEVER BEEN PROMOTED AND HER EMPLOYER DOESN'T APPRECIATE HER ATTEMPTS TO BREAK THE GLASS CEILING.

THEY'RE SEXIST?

I WORK IN A GREENHOUSE.

SHE JUST CAN'T STOP THROWING ROCKS.

IT'S FUN TO BREAK THOSE LITTLE PANES.

I GET IT. STOP.

My strip is a good influence on the youngsters.

That organ was a pain to draw. I will not be doing that again. So enjoy it while it's here.

HELLO. I'M RAT AND I'M RUNNING FOR PRESIDENT.

RAT 2016

FACE IT...YOU DON'T HAVE A LOT OF GOOD CHOICES IN THIS ELECTION. SO VOTE FOR ME. BECAUSE IF ELECTED, I PROMISE TO DO ONE THING.

ONE

THING

I will hand out free beer helmets to everyone.

THIS WILL LOOK GENEROUS. BUT IT IS A RUSE.

RAT 2016

Because the helmets of stupid people will be magnetized.

And when they are out enjoying their beer helmet, a giant magnetic crane will lift them off the street.

7/31

And drop them safely on the giant trash heap that floats in the Pacific.

We'll be rid of stupid people.
And stupid people will think they won a Hawaiian vacation.

A CRANE JUST PUT ME HERE.

ALOHA.

WON'T STUPID PEOPLE READ THIS AND BE ALERTED?

GOOD NEWS: THEY DON'T READ.

I'M FLYING! I'M FLYING!

There really is a giant trash heap floating in the Pacific. Don't vacation there.

Slightly related story: One time I went out drinking in Philadelphia with *Loose Parts* cartoonist Dave Blazek. When the night was over, he dropped me back off at my hotel. And as he drove off, I realized I left my phone in his car. I immediately thought of a brilliant plan: to call my cell phone, alerting him to the fact that it was in the car. But the phone battery was dead, so it would not have rung. Also, I didn't have a phone, as it was in Dave's car. Lesson to be learned here: Don't party with Dave Blazek.

I always write the strip to music. And for many years, my playlists would begin with the NWA song "Straight Outta Compton."

Panel 1: HEY NEIGHBOR NANCY. HOW GOES IT.?

NOT WELL. I HAD TO END AN AFFAIR I WAS HAVING WITH A GUY.

Panel 2: HOW COME.?

BECAUSE HE WAS SO PARANOID ABOUT GETTING CAUGHT. HE THOUGHT EVERYONE WAS ALWAYS LOOKING FOR HIM.

Panel 3: WHY DID HE FEEL THAT WAY.?

Panel 4: I HAVE MY REASONS.

See, this entire book is just one giant *Where's Waldo?* book. And you just found him.

Panel 1: WHO'S THE LITTLE GUY.?

MY DOG 'LIBIDO.' HE WANTS TO RUN AROUND FREE IN THE YARD.

RINNGG

Panel 2: HI, PIG...IT'S ME, PIGITA. DO YOU WANT TO COME OVER FOR A WHILE.?

SURE. BUT MY LIBIDO REALLY NEEDS TO BE UNLEASHED.

Panel 3: MAYBE YOU SHOULD STAY HOME.

YOU'RE VERY FICKLE.

You can stop reading now. You found Waldo.

Panel 1: I'M THINKING ABOUT OPENING A 10,000 SEAT OUTDOOR CONCERT VENUE ON OUR BLOCK.

Panel 2: YOU CAN'T DO THAT. THIS IS A RESIDENTIAL NEIGHBORHOOD. AT A MINIMUM, YOU'D HAVE TO FILE AN ENVIRONMENTAL IMPACT REPORT.

I DID. HAVE A LOOK.

Panel 3: THERE WILL BE NOISE.

Panel 4: COULD YOU ADD A LITTLE MORE DETAIL.?

LOTSA NOISE.

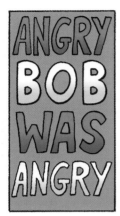
ANGRY BOB WAS ANGRY

"I am stressed out by financial troubles," thought Bob to himself. "And I must do something to relax."

So Bob took a class on transcendental meditation.

"Sit in a calm, quiet space for twenty minutes a day," said his spiritual guru. "And repeat a brief mantra to yourself."

So Bob went home. And for twenty minutes a day, he sat in a calm, quiet place and repeated his mantra.

And after one month, he was more stressed than ever.

"I do not understand," said his spiritual guru. "At this point, your spiritual energy should be in harmony with the universe. What, if I may ask, is your mantra?"

8/7

"Financially broke failure," said Bob.

Bob was kicked out of meditation class.

MEDITATION'S NOT FOR EVERYONE.

One of my friends recently started meditating. I asked him what his mantra was, but he said he had to keep it secret. I found that very annoying. So I'm gonna reveal that the friend in question was my stupid friend Emilio.

161

I was a lawyer for many years. And when I would get bored, I would sometimes just sit at my desk and draw. And presto, I went on to become a syndicated cartoonist. The lesson here: Screw off at your job and good things will happen.

My research shows that tofu does not actually come from a dead animal.

I love doing strips like this. Mostly because I know they drive sensitive readers nuts.

A mulligan is when you don't count a bad shot in golf. Or maybe you already knew that. The problem is I don't know who you are and how smart you might be. So go ahead and circle one of the following words that best describes you:

GENIUS   SMART   AVERAGE   BELOW AVERAGE   DUMB AS A PICKLE

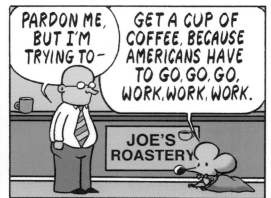

I don't know this for a fact, but I'm gonna guess that on the last strip you circled "DUMB AS A PICKLE."

Mike Scioscia is the manager of the Los Angeles Angels of Anaheim, which may be the longest team name in the history of sports. Personally, I think they should have added even more cities. Make it the Los Angeles Angels of Anaheim North of San Diego and West of Phoenix. Though that would be hard to fit on a uniform.

All true. So don't get too attached to whatever room you're sitting in right now.

165

Fun game: One of the houses is not like the others. See if you can find it.

Answer to last game: The first one. It's the only one with a brown couch.

Comment on last game: Shame on you if you thought it was the second one with the chimney.

RAT'S **SOCIAL CUES** for the **SOCIALLY INEPT**

EASY TO CUT OUT AND CARRY!

AND THEN...

You may talk too much.

Shirts cannot be worn six days in a row.

Hey. It's me.

Met u at bar.

Hey. It's me again.

Hey. Wassup?

Hey u.

She doesn't want to talk to you.

THANKSGIVING CANCELED.

You do not bring added joy to the holidays.

CRACK

That pick-up line was not effective.

8/21

MOTHER'S DAY LUNCHEON

My son did not fulfill expectations.

PRETTY BRILLIANT, HUH?

I've told this story before, but it bears repeating:

One time I was on a long flight with *Doonesbury* cartoonist Garry Trudeau. I was so excited to be sitting next to him that I asked him a ton of questions about his strip. After the twentieth or so question, I noticed he didn't answer. So I looked over at him and saw why. He had put on noise-canceling headphones.

This was another strip inspired by the syndicated cartoonist who told me he might have been put on earth by aliens.

This strange-looking eye was a doodle in my notebook. So I cut-and-pasted it into a strip and wrote a joke around it.

August 24 really is National Waffle Day. We should get that day off work.

Suddenly, Pig is spelling like the crocs. Perhaps I mixed up my characters here.

8/28

Bonus points if you noticed the headphone cord isn't connected to anything.

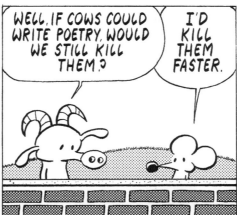

Looking back on this strip, I think it might have been funnier if I'd taken Rat's line from the second panel ("I'd kill them faster") and moved it to the third panel, eliminating the "snooty cows" comment. The reason I didn't do that originally is that I'm often cautious about ending on the joke, in case the joke doesn't land. So I put that extra line after it, almost like a safety net. But sometimes that extra line can screw up the bluntness of the original joke. Always a hard call.

Hey, the cows are writing like the crocs now, too. Those crocs are very influential.

Anne Meara was also the mother of Ben Stiller. I tell you that not to be informative, but because I have nothing else to say.

I like how I use the speech balloons to hide the sign in the first panel. I also like how I just complimented myself.

9/4

This I say with confidence: No one on the American comics page had ever before said the line "Visualize your cervix opening."

I'm old enough to remember this. What was especially strange was that they had "smoking sections" and "nonsmoking sections," as though the smoke didn't waft throughout the cabin.

I am.

I judge whether I am going to like someone by how many of their Facebook photos involve them making the peace sign. More than two: Bad person.

We could all use one of these rooms.

I have a friend who's involved in education. I told him I wanted to do this strip, and he gave me all of the terms that bug him.

In the right hands, that could be a very kinky housewarming gift.

True, Embarrassing Fact: I once played *Pokémon Go* so intently that I found myself on a private road heading toward what turned out to be a women's shelter. A very tough-looking woman met me halfway down the road and told me I needed to leave. I asked if I could get the Pokémon first. She said no.

The publisher of this very book publishes many adult coloring books. They would like you to know that there is nothing wrong with that.

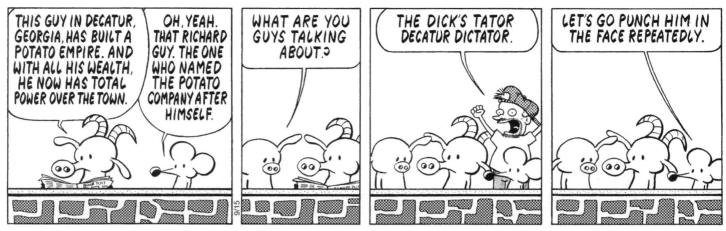

I recently rented a car and drove all through Georgia: Athens, Macon, Warm Springs, and Madison. I wanted to see Athens because that is where R.E.M. is from. And I wanted to see Macon because Little Richard's boyhood house is there. And I wanted to see Warm Springs because that's where Franklin Roosevelt died. But I didn't know why I was in Madison—so I just slept in my car.

We recently bought a couch that turns into a bed. But the bed is not comfortable. So when we have guests, I give them that bed.

PIG TOOK A TEST CALLED 'AWAY.' HE NEEDS IT IN ORDER TO BECOME A TRAVEL ADVISER.

THOSE GUYS MAKE A LOT OF MONEY. WHEN DOES HE FIND OUT HOW HE DID?

ANY MINUTE. I'M WAITING FOR HIS CALL.

THERE HE IS NOW.

RINNNG

I DID IT! I PASSED!

PIG PASSED AWAY! HE PASSED AWAY!!

THIS IS A VERY SICK COMIC STRIP.

I wonder how many bald men I've drawn in *Pearls*. It has to be in the thousands.

HEY, PIG, WHAT ARE YOU DOING?

I RECORDED ALL OF THE OLYMPICS AND I'M GONNA WATCH THIS ONE EVENT BECAUSE IT LOOKS THE MOST INTERESTING.

WHICH ONE IS IT?

THIS ONE WHERE THEY GIVE MEDALS FOR SHOWERING A LOT AND BEING RUDE.

THAT'S NOT WHAT THEY MEAN BY THE 'CLEAN AND JERK.'

THE 'BREAST STROKE'? HAVE THEY LOST ALL SENSE OF DECENCY?!

It is sort of interesting how I can say "breast stroke" but could never say "stroke breast."

WHAT'S ON YOUR SWEATER, PIG?

A MEANDERING BODY OF WATER. IT GOES RIGHT OVER THE SEAMS.

WHO MADE IT?

A SEAMSTRESS I KNOW. SHE USED A STEAM-POWERED SEWING MACHINE. BUT WHEN I PICKED IT UP, SHE LOOKED WORRIED ABOUT SOMETHING.

WHAT ARE YOU TALKING ABOUT?

THE STEAMED-SEAMED STREAM SEAMSTRESS SEEMED STRESSED.

HAVE YOU NOTHING BETTER TO DO?

HEY, PIGITA, I WAS THINKING WE SHOULD HAVE ONE OF OUR ROMANTIC NIGHTS.

WELL, PIG, I HAVE SOME LINGERI—

LINGERIE?

LINGERING DOUBTS ABOUT OUR RELATIONSHIP.

LANGUAGE IS CRUEL.

Someone pointed out that this strip doesn't work because of the way "lingerie" is pronounced. The beginning of the word doesn't sound like the beginning of "lingering." That's true, but in terms of spelling, the beginning of the two words is exactly the same. So I guess this is dependent on whether or not you "hear" the words as you read them.

NO MATTER HOW HARD YOU TRY, SYNCHRONIZED EATING WILL NEVER BE AN OLYMPIC EVENT.

YOU NEVER KNOW.

I LOVE THE PRACTICE.

CHOMP CHOMP CHOMP   CHOMP CHOMP CHOMP

9/22

DID YOU EVER NOTICE THAT THE RETURN NETFLIX ENVELOPE IS ADDRESSED TO THE 'NEAREST NETFLIX SHIPPING FACILITY'?

YEAH. SO?

SO COULD I ADDRESS A LETTER TO THE 'NEAREST HOT WOMAN'?

NO.

'DEAR HOT WOMAN... YOU'RE PROBABLY WONDERING HOW I FOUND YOU...'

9/23

Question for everyone: Is it just me, or do a good portion of your Netflix DVDs appear to have been run over by elephants on roller skates?

NEIGHBOR BOB CAME BY AND GAVE US A GIFT.

I DON'T TRUST THAT GUY. ARE THERE ANY STRINGS ATTACHED?

NO.

ALRIGHT, THEN. WHAT IS IT?

A GUITAR.

IT'S HARD TO PLAY.

9/24

This strip is rather bad. Instead of reading it, please just turn the page.

Rat's Guide to People You Can Do Without

Very handy.

The guy whose every Facebook post is sadder than the last.

Joe T.

Dog died. Grandpa died. House burned down.

Like   Comment   Share

The fat guy in the aisle seat who unapologetically takes both arm rests.

No worries. I'll just make myself into a toothpick.

The neighbor who thinks they need to alert you to everything.

Just so you know, I saw a guy walking on the street. He was tall.

The friend who peppers his language with words he barely knows.

I have a plethora of loquacious bees.

The aunt who forwards every health-related email on the internet.

To: Nephew Bob
From: Aunt Hilda
Subject: SIGNS OF A STROKE
DO NOT DELETE!!!!

The cartoonist who pretends to have one of his characters draw his strip because he's too lazy to draw a real one.

HI

WHOA WHOA WHOA.

TRUTH HURTS.

THIS IS SO DARN PLETHORA.

Cartooning Rule No. 402: When you don't know how to properly draw caricatures of political figures, just show a small amount of their podiums and call it a day.

See above rule.

An Olympic neighbor is at least better than a census neighbor. Those you need to see only once a decade.

There is no defending the spelling of "colonel." It bears no relation to how the word is pronounced.

Fifty Shades of Green

by Larry

"You is smell gud," say Larry.

"And you smoove curves. Me luv dem."

"You. Are. Mine," growl Larry.

"And me gonna run my mouf all over you body parts."

10/2

MUST YOU TALK SO MUCH EVERY TIME WE GET A BUCKET OF CHICKEN?

Wife no unnerstand me.

After reading this strip, you might be asking yourself, "Isn't it rather lazy of Stephan to have absolutely no drawings in four of the seven panels?" And I might be answering, "Yep."

185

Every year or so, I auction a couple strips for charity. To get announcements about the auctions (as well as many other things), just go to facebook.com/pearlscomic.

Making fun of Congress is great because their approval rating is 14 percent. In one poll, both traffic jams and colonoscopies had higher approval ratings.

You might be wondering how Pig's bow tie stays attached, given that it's not tied around his neck and has nothing to clip on to. I'm wondering that also.

I recently traveled to Peru, where I tried my best to speak Spanish. But whenever I couldn't come up with a word, I would just take the English word and add an "o" to the end of it. Sometimes it actually worked. Though I will give you this helpful tip: *hando* is not the word for "hand."

I often use Beatles lyrics for these puns because I've found that their lyrics are known by just about everybody. Also, that almost kinda looks like Ringo Starr. So no need to draw just a portion of a podium for that guy.

DID YOU KNOW THAT BIG, GIANT GREENLAND IS A TERRITORY OF TINY, LITTLE DENMARK, AND THAT DENMARK IS RESPONSIBLE FOR ITS DEFENSE?

SO?

SO LET'S INVADE GREENLAND!

IT'S HIS NEW CAMPAIGN ISSUE.

IT'S MOSTLY ICE.

GOOD NEWS. GLOBAL WARMING IS CHANGING THAT.

No Greenlandtonians complained.

SIR, IS IT TRUE THAT YOUR PRESIDENTIAL CAMPAIGN IS NOW BASED ON ONE ISSUE— THE INVASION OF GREENLAND?

YES. IT'S A TERRITORY OF THE DANES. AND THEY WON'T SEE IT COMING.

BUT WHY GREEN-LAND?

BECAUSE IT'S EIGHT TIMES THE SIZE OF GREAT BRITAIN, BUT ONLY HAS 57,000 PEOPLE, WHICH IS NOT MUCH MORE THAN SARASOTA, FLORIDA.

I SEE. SO BY THAT LOGIC, WHY NOT JUST INVADE SARASOTA, FLORIDA?

WELL, NOW, THERE'S AN IDEA.

AND SADLY, HE'S STILL BETTER THAN THE OTHER TWO CAND-IDATES.

SARASOTA, YOUR RETIREMENT COMMUNITIES ARE MINE!

Regarding the last strip, I am informed by reliable sources that the proper term for people from Greenland is "Greenlanders." So if you go there, please don't refer to them as "Greenlandtonians."

I SAW A GIRL TODAY WEARING SWEATPANTS WITH THE WORD 'PEACE' PRINTED ON THE BUTT.

SO?

SO IT GAVE ME AN IDEA.

MY BUTT PROPAGANDA TAKES A BACKSEAT TO NO ONE.

EXCUSE ME, MR. PHONE COMPANY GUY...YOU LEFT THIS PHONEBOOK ON MY PORCH, BUT NO ONE USES THEM ANYMORE.

NOT TRUE.

WHAT DO YOU MEAN?

IF COPS NEED TO BEAT SOMEONE THEY'RE INTERROGATING, THEY USE A PHONEBOOK BECAUSE IT DOESN'T LEAVE MARKS. SO IF YOU EVER BECOME A COP, THAT THING COULD BE PRETTY HELPFUL.

IT'S NICE TO SEE THE PHONE COMPANY ADAPTING.

I have learned over the last few years that any strip that touches upon police conduct is guaranteed to anger a few oversensitive folk. Here's my solution: Be less sensitive.

I THINK THE KEY TO SUCCESS IN LIFE IS TO TRUST YOUR GUT.

I DO THAT.

YOU DO?

YES. I TRUST THAT IT WILL ALWAYS BE THERE.

I THINK THAT'S DIFFERENT.

IT'S THE MOST TRUSTWORTHY PART OF ME.

How in the world do these short characters get up on those tall diner stools? I should think about these things before I draw them.

WHERE YOU OFF TO, GOAT?

FLOWER MARKET.

WHAT DO THEY SELL THERE?

PIG, JUST LISTEN TO THE WORDS...FLOWER...MARKET...SO THE ANSWER IS FLOWERS. THEY SELL FLOWERS.

SO THE FLEA MARKET MUST BE AN AWFUL PLACE.

Look at the woman in the purple shirt in Panel 1. Then look at the same woman in Panel 6. She has grown considerably. Perhaps she ate quite a bit between panels.

This entire series was suggested by a reader.

When my strip first started in 2002, I could not say the word "sucks." Now I can. And it is very exciting.

I actually took both the brick wall and TV scenes from Charles Schulz's *Peanuts*, although I believe his characters sat on beanbags.

I first drew Rat when I was in law school. And at the time, he stood on all four legs. Only later did he stand upright on two feet.

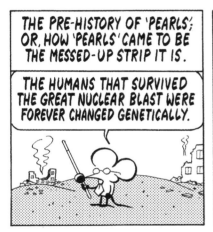

When you draw a comic strip character, 90 percent of their expression comes from a combination of their eyes and their mouth. But the tone of my strip is generally understated (that is, dry). So by removing the mouths, I think it better fits that tone. It's sort of the opposite of the humor in 1940s-era comics, most of which had very expressive eyes and mouths and a whole lot of exclamation points.

10/23

Strange but True Fact: Taco Bell actually tried to open locations in Mexico, but it failed. All the outlets were closed within two years.

I had a friend who told me all the problems he and his wife were having in trying to adopt. I wrote this in response to that.

Marijuana is legal in Oregon. This has nothing to do with my many, many trips to Oregon.

I have a friend who works at Nike's headquarters. He asked for the original of this strip, and I sent it to him.

This comment is not about this strip. It's about the next one.

It's bad. Embarrassingly bad. So promise me you will skip it and go on to the next one.

You read it anyway. I'm disappointed.

WHAT ARE YOU DOING, PIG?

IT'S MY HALLOWEEN COSTUME.

WHAT IS IT?

IT'S A GIANT PUPPY EYE. IT'S FROM THAT STATUE OF A PUPPY ON TOP OF BOW WOW BURGERS.

AND IT FELL OFF?

YEAH, SO I THOUGHT I'D USE IT FOR A COSTUME.

YOU FELT YOU HAD THE RIGHT TO JUST TAKE IT?

IT DREW ME IN. LIKE A GIANT LURE.

LURE?

LURE. LURE. LURE. LURE. LURE. LURE.

THAT'S RIDICULOUS. THE COSTUME DOESN'T EVEN MAKE SENSE. WHAT ARE YOU EVEN SUPPOSED TO BE?

I'M PUP EYE THE SAY 'LURE' MAN.

YOU'VE RUINED HALLOWEEN.

197

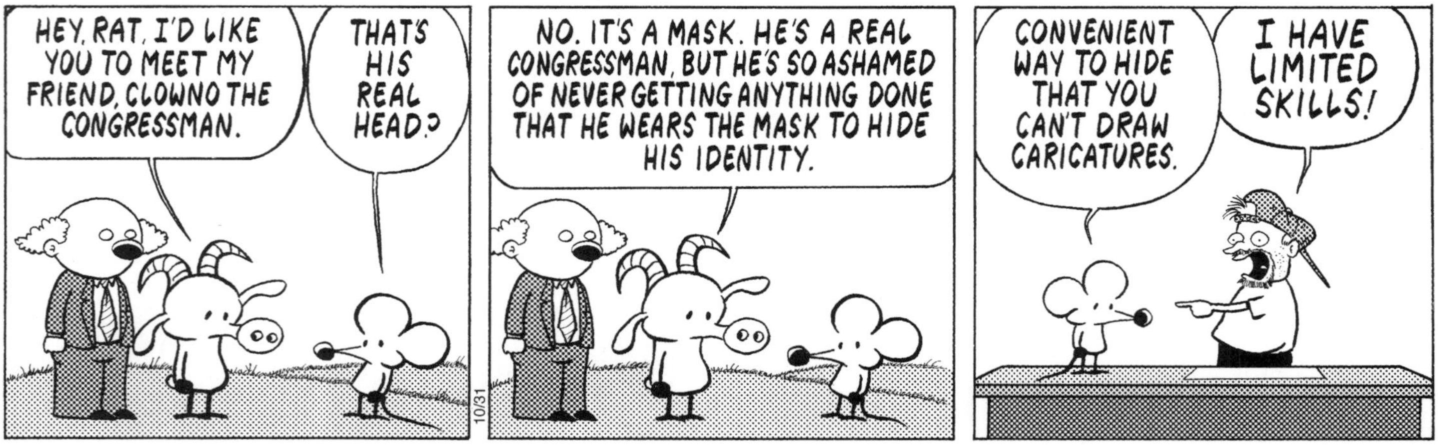
HEY, RAT, I'D LIKE YOU TO MEET MY FRIEND, CLOWNO THE CONGRESSMAN.
THAT'S HIS REAL HEAD?
NO. IT'S A MASK. HE'S A REAL CONGRESSMAN, BUT HE'S SO ASHAMED OF NEVER GETTING ANYTHING DONE THAT HE WEARS THE MASK TO HIDE HIS IDENTITY.
CONVENIENT WAY TO HIDE THAT YOU CAN'T DRAW CARICATURES.
I HAVE LIMITED SKILLS!

Yes, but I draw a mean Ringo Starr.

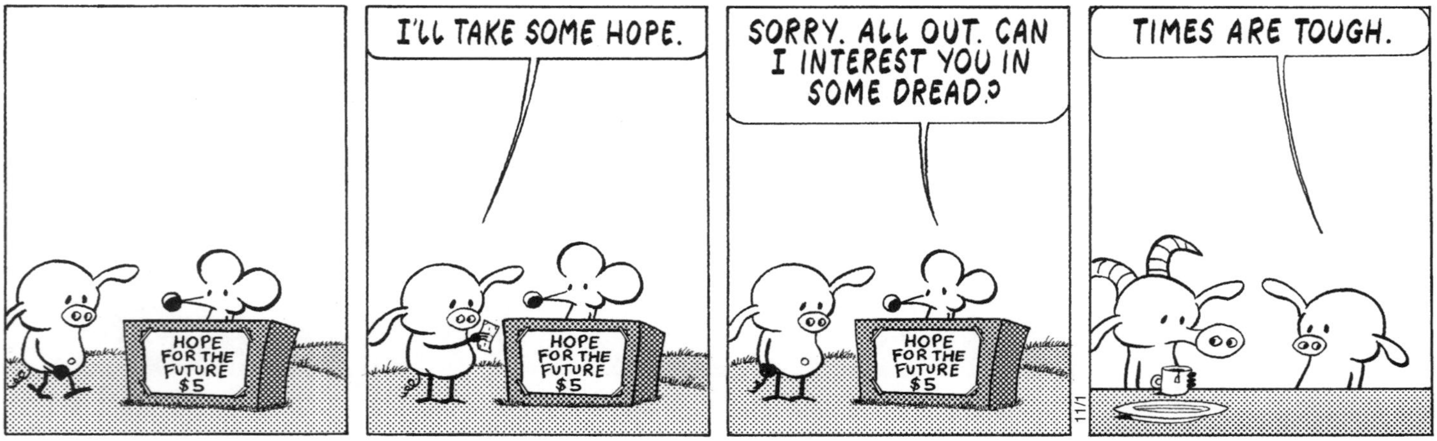
HOPE FOR THE FUTURE $5
I'LL TAKE SOME HOPE.
SORRY. ALL OUT. CAN I INTEREST YOU IN SOME DREAD?
TIMES ARE TOUGH.

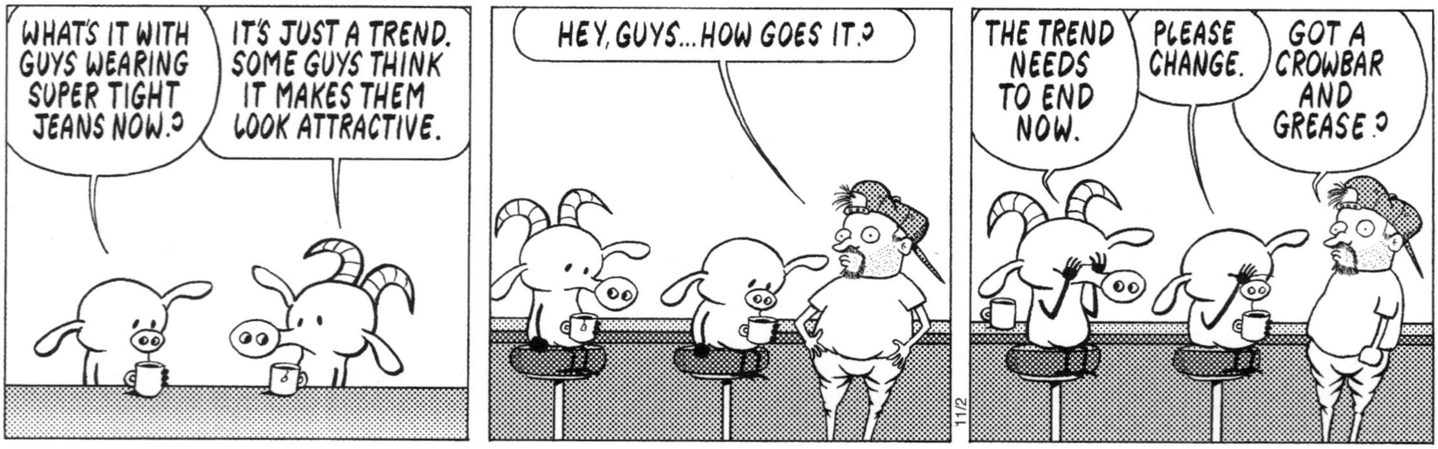
WHAT'S IT WITH GUYS WEARING SUPER TIGHT JEANS NOW?
IT'S JUST A TREND. SOME GUYS THINK IT MAKES THEM LOOK ATTRACTIVE.
HEY, GUYS... HOW GOES IT?
THE TREND NEEDS TO END NOW.
PLEASE CHANGE.
GOT A CROWBAR AND GREASE?

I actually tried on a pair of these jeans once. Please don't share that with anyone.

For me, a place that only has seats at a communal table is like a place that doesn't have any seats at all.

They don't wear paper bags. But I recently bought my son one of those Mexican wrestler masks, and he's been wearing it when he's with me.

EXCEPT IN ARIZONA, WHICH DOESN'T OBSERVE IT. SO WHEN YOU GET TO PHOENIX, THE HOUR YOU JUST WENT BACK IN TEXAS GETS UNDONE, PLUS YOU HAVE THE HOUR BEHIND FOR THE TIME ZONE, WHICH—

11/6

WHO NEEDS WATCHES?

On my last book tour, I did a signing in Dallas, and it was the only time I ever had an armed bodyguard standing at my side throughout a signing. I don't know why he was there, but it made me feel very powerful.

I'm hoping you didn't really Google image it. But if you did, I hope it was educational.

I recently did a charity event in Boise, Idaho, where I discovered a restaurant that was just called "Bacon," because it served bacon. While that's not weird, this next fact is: The host of the charity event was named Jeff Bacon.

WHO ARE YOU?

HUMOR POLICE. FROM NOW ON, I'LL BE DECIDING WHAT'S FUNNY AND WHAT'S NOT.

WHAT DO YOU THINK IS FUNNY?

EVERYTHING. AS LONG AS IT DOESN'T INVOLVE RACE, ETHNICITY, RELIGION, POLITICS, SEXUAL ORIENTATION, GENDER, TRANSGENDER, OBSCENITY, BODY-SHAMING, AGE-ISM, THE DISABLED, LITTLE PEOPLE, VEGETARIANS, THE GLUTEN-INTOLERANT, OPINIONS, TRUTH, OR CRUELTY TO DOLPHINS.

WOULDN'T IT BE QUICKER TO LIST THE JOKES WE CAN MAKE?

THE CHICKEN CROSSING THE ROAD ONE.

HAHAHA HAHAHA I LOVE THAT ONE!

I've never gotten in trouble for dolphin jokes, but *Pearls* was once canceled from a newspaper in Oklahoma for a strip where Rat threw a little person off a pier.

WHO'S YOUR FAVORITE ACTRESS?

ELLEN BURSTYN. AND I HEARD SHE LIKED CHESTNUTS, SO I SENT HER 2,000 POUNDS OF THEM THAT I PICKED OFF TREES.

WOW. AREN'T THOSE COVERED IN TINY BURRS?

YEAH, BUT SHE REMOVED THE BURRS AND BLEW THEM ALL UP TO GET RID OF THEM.

BURSTYN BURST ONE BURRS TON?

YOU ARE A BURR IN THE SADDLE OF LIFE.

Speaking of saddles, I have ridden a horse only once. The moment I got on it, it ran as fast as it could away from the stables. This proved to me that all horses are possessed by Satan.

WHERE YOU OFF TO?

TO PROTEST THE AMOUNT OF VIOLENCE IN MOVIES.

ENOUGH

GOOD FOR YOU. THERE'S FAR TOO MUCH.

TOO LITTLE.

ENOUGH

IF THEY DISAGREE, I'LL HIT THEM WITH THE SIGN.

ENOUGH

11/13

I just returned from my first trip to Mexico City. While there, I sat in the front row of a Mexican wrestling match. During one of the matches, a fake tooth flew out of the ring and broke my sunglasses. That's when you know you have a good seat.

I find it hard to believe I ruin the *entire* comics page. After all, there are all those dumb soap opera ones.

I really do camp out at the café where I currently write the strip, sometimes sitting there for as much as four hours. They must hate me.

We have deer at our house that eat all our plants. It has made me much less sympathetic toward Bambi.

It's a wonder my family is not as fond of my work as I am.

TODAY I'D LIKE TO LOOK AT MATTHEW 16:26...'FOR WHAT WILL IT PROFIT A MAN IF HE GAINS THE WHOLE WORLD, BUT FORFEITS HIS SOUL?'

INDEED.

IS IT THE GOAL OF LIFE TO AMASS AS MUCH MONEY AS ONE POSSIBLY CAN?

IS IT THE GOAL OF LIFE TO OWN THE BIGGEST HOUSE?

IS IT THE GOAL OF LIFE TO IMPRESS YOUR NEIGHBOR WITH THE NICEST CAR, THE BEST CLOTHES, THE FANCIEST WATCH?

11/20

YES! YES! YES!

GUESS HE DIDN'T REALLY WANT AN ANSWER.

I'VE NEVER SEEN A CHURCH EJECTION BEFORE.

I've never been ejected from a church, but I was ejected from a Little League game when I was eight. I'm proud of that.

Write a strip on this subject and you will find out from newspaper readers more than you ever wanted to know about whether it's "duct" or "duck" tape.

As a graduate of the University of California, I take every chance I get to make fun of my school's rival, Stanford, which we lovingly misspell "Stanfurd."

I once milked a cow when I was a little kid. That's not particularly interesting, but I had nothing else to say here.

Oh, and one more thing about that last cow-milking comment. On the same day I milked the cow, I grabbed an electric fence. You may excuse that as the idiocy of a child. But 30 years later, when I was 40, I grabbed another one. So it's just plain idiocy.

This was based on a true event. It's amazing what banks can get away with.

This was one of the most popular strips of the year.

This strip was a big hit in Boise. Both the local newspaper and one of the TV news stations did stories about it. I later auctioned the strip for a Boise charity, and it sold for $5,000. You may also notice the name "Julia Pastis" in the margin. She's my daughter, and I had her put her name there because she helped me ink the strip.

On a recent trip to Mexico City, I visited the former house of the Russian revolutionary Leon Trotsky. The house was the site of a failed assassination attempt where gunmen tried to shoot him through a window. As a result, Trotsky bricked over his kitchen window. But it didn't matter, because he was later killed by a guy with an ice pick. It's always something.

This might have helped Trotsky.

HOW ARE YOUR EGGS, DAD?

RUNNY. BUT I GUESS THEY'RE FINE.

SORRY. THIS WAS THE ONLY PLACE I COULD TAKE YOU FOR BREAKFAST THAT WAS NEAR YOUR HOUSE.

YEAH, WELL, WITH THE TRAFFIC NOW, IT'S IMPOSSIBLE TO GO ANYWHERE.

JUST YESTERDAY, I HAD TO GET TO MY DOCTOR'S APPOINTMENT. MADE ME TEN MINUTES LATE.

OF COURSE, THAT STUPID DOCTOR IS ALWAYS LATE, TOO. HE'S TERRIBLE.

THE IDIOT DOESN'T EVEN KNOW WHAT THIS PAIN IN MY LEG IS.

HURTS. ALL THE TIME. PAIN, PAIN, PAIN, PAIN. IT'S HORRIBLE.

12/4

NOW MY G☆#G COFFEE'S COLD.

AND WHY DON'T YOU TAKE ME TO BREAKFAST MORE OFTEN?

'CAUSE... LIFE... NOT... WORTH... LIVING.

This is loosely based on my own dad. I can safely say that because he doesn't read these books. And if he does, I deny everything.

If I were to rank my favorite pizza toppings, I think I would put olives last. Pepperoni would be first, followed closely by pineapple. And yes, I admitted I like pineapple.

The trunk of my wife's car has one of these buttons. And I use it every time.

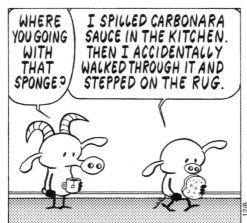

THERE IS NOTHING WRONG WITH PINEAPPLE ON PIZZA!

But there is something wrong with anchovies. You should not befriend anyone who likes anchovies.

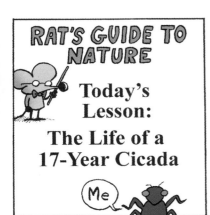

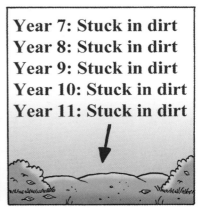

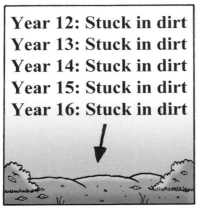

They really do live in the dirt for 17 years. As our president would say: SAD!

EVERY HEADSTONE, EVERY BOOK, EVERY SCULPTURE, EVERY SONG, EVERY BUILDING, EVERY AWARD, ARE ALL JUST THE SAME THING... THE INDIVIDUAL CRYING, 'I WAS HERE.'

AND YET EVERY ONE OF US, GIVEN THE PASSAGE OF ENOUGH TIME, IS FORGOTTEN.

SO DRINK BEER, 'CAUSE SOON YOU'LL BE DEAD.

NOT QUITE WHAT I WAS GOING FOR.

EMBRACE THE VOID.

I like Rat's line in the third panel. Maybe I'll make it a book title.

I'M GOING ON A DATE WITH PIGITA TONIGHT. I THINK THINGS MIGHT GET PRETTY ROMANTIC.

WELL, MAKE SURE YOU BRING PROTECTION.

YOU THINK THAT'S IMPORTANT?

OF COURSE.

FRIENDS OF YOURS?

DON'T GET TOO CLOSE.

I FEEL TERRIBLE ABOUT MYSELF TODAY... MY LACK OF DRIVE... MY LACK OF SELF-DISCIPLINE... MY LACK OF SUCCESS.

WELL, GO OUT AND DO SOMETHING ABOUT IT.

YOU'RE RIGHT.

GOOD.

I'LL GO ON THE INTERNET AND HEAP SCORN ON COMPLETE STRANGERS.

NO.

AHHH... THE JOYS OF ANONYMITY.

I am often asked if I read the comments below my strip at pearlscomic.com. I do not. Once you've done a strip for 16 years, you have a pretty good idea what the range of opinions about you are.

Panel 1: THIS CHURCH IS MAKING IT REALLY EASY TO GET ORDAINED AS A PRIEST. THEY LET YOU DO IT ONLINE.

Panel 2: IS THAT A GOOD THING? / I DON'T KNOW. I GUESS IT DEPENDS ON WHAT KIND OF PEOPLE APPLY.

Panel 3: BLESS YOU, MY SON. / IT'S A BAD THING.

Rat is so easy to write for.

Panel 1: WHAT ARE YOU DOING? / FORGIVING SINS FOR CASH. (Sins Forgiven $5.00)

Panel 2: THAT'S NOT ETHICAL.

Panel 3: (silent)

Panel 4: I'M FORGIVEN.

Panel 1: PIG, WHY ARE YOUR FINGERS ORANGE? / FROM EATING CHEESE PUFFS.

Panel 2: WHY DON'T YOU JUST WASH YOUR HANDS? / IT'S PERMANENT.

Panel 3: GET HELP. / THERE ARE NO REHAB CLINICS FOR PUFFAHOLICS!!

I don't know what it is about cheese puffs. But if I start eating them, I literally cannot stop until there is not a single one left in the bag or anywhere else in the house. I believe they're more powerful than crack.

IT'S A WONDERFUL *PEARLS* LIFE

by S. T. Pastis

VERY HEART-WARMING

LIFE IS TERRIBLE. I'M GONNA JUMP AND END IT ALL....

WAIT! WAIT! WAIT!

WHO SAID THAT?

CLARENCE, YOUR GUARDIAN ANGEL, HERE TO SHOW YOU WHAT WOULD HAVE HAPPENED HAD YOU NEVER LIVED.

LIKE HERE, LOOK AT YOUR GOOD PAL, PIG... HE DOESN'T HAVE YOU AROUND IN HIS LIFE... SO HE'S ALL ALONE.

SO HE HAS TO MAKE OTHER FRIENDS, BUT THEY'RE NOT LIKE YOU. AND SUDDENLY, HE'S SELF-CONFIDENT AND HAPPY, AND HIS HAPPINESS SPREADS.

12/18

AND THE ENTIRE WORLD IS AT PEACE AND THE MIDDLE EAST IS CALM AND ALL RACES AND CREEDS LIVE TOGETHER IN BROTHERHOOD.

SO YOU SHOULD PROBABLY JUMP.

NO WAY. I HAVE A SICKENINGLY SWEET WORLD TO DISRUPT.

In the entire history of the strip, I think I've showed it snowing only two or three times. Maybe it's because I live in California and have seen snow fall only a couple times in my life.

If you know that song, it is now stuck in your head for the rest of today.

You will never meet someone who cares less about cars than me. I have an old Honda Accord and will continue to have it for as long as it will run. Plus, the ladies can't resist a man cruising around in a four-door Accord.

The "brown-nose" reindeer joke was one I used way back in the early days of the strip, before it ran in many newspapers. So I sort of stole the joke from myself. I have since hired a lawyer.

I find the reclining of airline seats to truly be a test of the goodness of mankind. And so far, mankind's failing.

A lot of people seemed to like this strip. A rare, touchy-feely one.

I heard once that driverless cars have to be programmed to make value judgments. In other words, if the situation arises and there are no alternatives, it has to decide whether to run over a bike, a dog, or a telemarketer. I assume it picks the telemarketer.

Forgive her, Google, for she has sinned.

GOALS FOR THE UPCOMING YEAR:

Sleep in more.

Remain fat.

IT'S IMPORTANT TO SET REALISTIC GOALS.

I frequently post my strips on Twitter (@stephanpastis), and this one was one of the most retweeted strips of the year.

HEY, RAT. I'M HOME.

WHERE WERE YOU?

BIG SALE. THE COUNTY WAS SELLING ALL THEIR SURPLUS CLOTHING.

OH, YEAH? WHICH COUNTY DEPARTMENT?

I'M NOT SURE.

My cousin Vincent was born on June 10. Hence the number on Pig's prison uniform.

WHAT ARE YOU DOING, TONIGHT?

I'M GONNA GET INTO MY WARM BED AND READ THIS NEW BOOK I GOT FOR CHRISTMAS.

OR INSTEAD OF DOING THAT, I MIGHT GO OUT IN THE COLD AND STAY UP LATE WITH STRANGERS WHO ARE FIGHTING AND THROWING UP, SO I CAN STARE AT THE CLOCK AT 11:59 P.M. AND PRETEND THAT MIDNIGHT CHANGES EVERYTHING.

YOU LEFT OUT THE FUNNY GLASSES.

OH, LOOK, IT'S BEDTIME.

I was a lawyer for almost ten years. Then I became a syndicated cartoonist and was able to quit. So yes, reach for the sky.

This strip sort of flows nicely from the last one. Sometimes stuff like that just happens by accident.

Surprisingly, this strip confused a few people who didn't know that "hump" was a synonym for sex. And for all you kids out there, please just skip over that last sentence.

When I was a lawyer, I took a lot of depositions. A deposition is when you ask a person questions under oath, usually with another attorney present. And, typically, there is a whole lot of arguing between attorneys. I always felt sorry for the court reporter who had to sit through all that.

If you look at the beginning of that curse word, I pretty clearly telegraph what the word is.

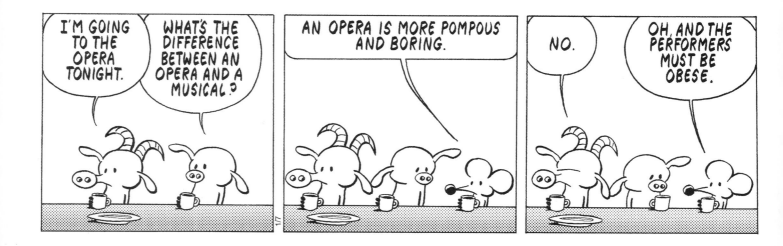

This is totally me. I start watching those videos on that Facebook feed and I can't stop.

The best part about being a cartoonist is that no one can tell you what time you have to get up. Except your wife. There's always the wife.

This strip came from a conversation I was having with a couple at a bar in Key West, Florida. I said I had been to a "tapas" bar, and they misheard me and asked, "Topless?" And, thus, a strip was born.

Maybe it's me, but "$#$# happens" would be a pretty great sympathy card.

Dear Beloved Friend,
I know this message will come to you as surprised. I am prince in Nigeria. There are great sums in U.S. America bank. I am here seeking avenue transfer funds to you.

WHY DO SCAMMERS STILL BOTHER TO SEND THESE POORLY WORDED, OBVIOUSLY FRAUDULENT EMAILS?

MUST BE GUYS WHO DON'T KNOW HOW STUPID THEY SOUND.

Why no one answer?

I HEARD YOU JUST GOT BACK FROM YOUR TRIP OVERSEAS. HOW ARE THINGS?

TERRIBLE. I GOT REALLY SICK AND HAD TO GO TO A HOSPITAL WHERE THEY MADE ME WAIT EIGHT HOURS IN THE EMERGENCY ROOM.

THAT'S ONE OF THE RISKS OF TRAVELING IN POOR OVERSEAS COUNTRIES. YOU NEVER KNOW THE STATE OF THEIR EMERGENCY FACILITIES.

THAT HAPPENED HERE.

YOU SHOULD KNOW BETTER THAN TO GET SICK HERE.

I'M AVOIDING IT FROM NOW ON.

This strip came from a visit my nephew made to the emergency room in Northern California. He had to wait hours and hours. It seemed wrong, so I wrote a strip about it.

WHAT DO YOU HAVE THERE, PIG?

A USED CLOCK I JUST BOUGHT.

HOW DOES IT WORK?

THE MAN'S HEAD INDICATES THE HOUR. HIS RIGHT HAND INDICATES THE MINUTE. AND HIS OTHER HAND INDICATES THE SECONDS, BUT IT BROKE.

WHAT DO YOU EXPECT FROM A SECONDHAND SECOND HAND SECOND HAND?

SURELY YOU CAN RETURN TO YOUR LAW CAREER.

229

WHAT ARE YOU DOING, RAT?

TAKING A STAND. I JUST CAN'T LET THE WHOLE WORLD BE RUINED ANYMORE.

WELL, GOOD FOR YOU...WE ALL NEED TO START GETTING INVOLVED.

IN FACT, I THINK THE REASON WE HAVE SO MANY PROBLEMS TODAY IS THAT PEOPLE JUST DON'T PARTICIPATE IN THE SYSTEM ANYMORE.

THEY LET OTHER PEOPLE MAKE THE SIGNS AND GO TO THE RALLIES, AND THEY NEVER MAKE THEIR OWN VOICES HEARD.

AND WHAT BETTER ISSUE TO TAKE A STAND ON THAN THE ENVIRONMENT?

THE ENVIRONMENT?

SAVE OUR PLANET STOP GLOBAL WHINING

I TAKE IT ALL BACK.

I'M SAVING OUR WORLD!

GOAT'S A GLOBAL WHINING DENIER.

Global whining is very real.

Rat's philosophy here is my philosophy. Fate is just waiting for you to be happy so it can attack and ruin everything. Don't risk it.

As a cartoonist, I think it's better if people don't have a firm grasp on your beliefs. That way, they don't come to the strip with any preconceptions. They never know what to expect.

As I get older, the more I realize that Goat is right. But the Rat in me is not going down without a fight.

I liked this one. It sets things up so that most readers think I'm talking about Trump, only to reveal that Rat is the one who's been elected.

1/22

Holy heavens, did this confuse people. So let me clear things up:
Pig thinks Goat is saying "all of her."

MR. PRESIDENT, NOW THAT YOU'RE IN OFFICE, THIS IS A GREAT OPPORTUNITY TO SET FORTH YOUR POLICY PRIORITIES.

RIGHT. I'VE PUT THEM ALL IN HERE.

BUT THIS IS JUST FILLED WITH PEOPLE'S NAMES.

RIGHT. THEY'RE MY ENEMIES. CRUSHING THEM WILL BE MY PRIORITY.

I HOPED FOR SO MUCH MORE.

OH, WE CAN ADD TO IT AS WE GO.

Nixon had an enemies list. Rat has an enemies phone book.

PRESIDENT RAT IS ON T.V. LAYING OUT HIS PLAN FOR MASS DEPORTATION.

SO HE'S REALLY GONNA DEPORT ALL THE UNDOCUMENTED IMMIGRANTS?

I DON'T THINK THAT'S WHO HE'S GOING AFTER.

MEN WITH MAN BUNS, OUT!

I think we can all agree on this.

WHEW, AM I TIRED... BEEN TRAINING FOR A TRIATHLON. IT'S MY SIXTH TRIATHLON. I REALLY ENJOY TRIATHLONS.

LISTEN, TOMMY THE TRIATHLETE... NO ONE CARES ABOUT YOUR TRIATHLONS, BECAUSE WE ALL RECOGNIZE THAT WHAT YOU'RE REALLY SAYING IS THAT YOU'RE BETTER THAN US. SO JUST SAY IT.

I'M BETTER THAN YOU.

FEEL BETTER?

YOUR WHOLE, UNDISCIPLINED EXISTENCE IS WITHOUT VALUE!

Strips like this are my favorite. Simple. Good turn of a phrase.

This begins a sequence where I will just keep complimenting myself.

That's a very well-drawn colander. I'm quite the artist.

I like this joke. It's fairly brilliant.

Also brilliant. Good use of breaking the fourth wall. Well thought out.

Okay, even I've grown sick of complimenting myself. We return now to your regular programming.

I'm not sure this joke works. I think most people who read a little bit of what Goat's saying in the first panel probably realize those are bands.

For those who are not familiar with the term "randy," it means, well, lustful. And for those who knew what it meant, you should be ashamed of yourselves.

Now I'm wondering what's in there.

I am almost always at least six months ahead of deadline. Although if I want to do something topical, I can usually substitute it in for another strip.

Subtle political commentary. I'm very, very clever.

I've said it before, but it bears repeating. In all the times I've made fun of France and French people, not one of them has ever complained. This proves that they either have a great sense of humor or are too busy smoking cigarettes to care.

Any resemblance to our current president is purely coincidental. And if you hear otherwise, FAKE NEWS! SAD!

I must have very low self-esteem.

I'm usually risk-averse, but on a recent trip to Mexico City, I had a drink that contained tarantula venom. My whole mouth went numb. I'm now thinking that was not wise.

In 2017, Trump just dominated the zeitgeist. There was no way around it. To not comment on it as a humorist was to make your work almost irrelevant.

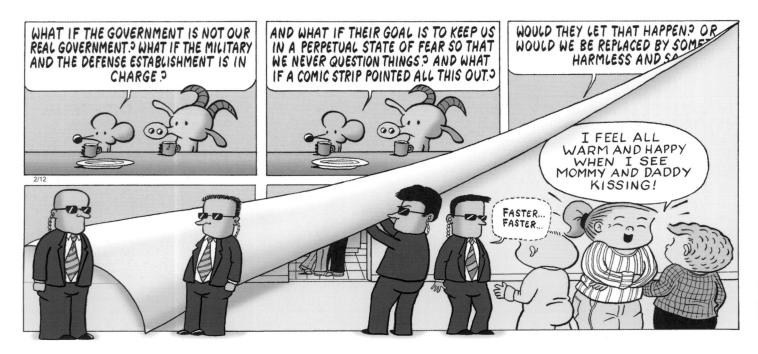

I like the way this strip turned out. Also, it's always fun to draw those little runts.

Those are all actual streets and places in Atlanta. They are obsessed with peaches. They should throw in a Banana Way now and then.

Matt Wuerker is a cartoonist for Politico. I met him once for drinks in Washington, D.C., and really liked him. So please don't kick him in the hoo-haws.

Panel 1: HEY, PIG, WHERE ARE YOU OFF TO? / THE MOVIES. WANT TO GO WITH ME?

Panel 2: WHO, ME? L'IL OL' ME? I MEAN, I'D LOVE TO, IF YOU REALLY WANTED ME TO, BUT I'M SURE YOU DON'T REALLY WANT THAT.

Panel 3: IT'S FINE. JUST STOP BEING COY.

Panel 4: HOW RACIST. / KOI POND

In 2009, a number of other cartoonists and I went on a USO trip to Iraq. While there, we got to stay in Saddam Hussein's palace. Though there were many amazing things about our time there, the thing I remember best is a man-made lake behind the palace that was filled with the largest koi I have ever seen. The soldiers gave us Cocoa Puffs to feed them. The koi practically crawled out of the pond to get the food, almost like quasi-alligators. All in the middle of a war. It was odd.

Panel 1: HAVE YOU EVER READ 'THE ROAD NOT TAKEN' BY ROBERT FROST? IT REALLY IS AN AMAZING POEM. / SURE. I KNOW THAT ONE.

Panel 2: 'TWO ROADS DIVERGED IN A WOOD AND I— I TOOK THE ONE LESS TRAVELED BY, AND MY CAR HIT A BIG G☆#G☆#G ROCK, AND I WAS STRANDED FOR SIX HOURS.'

Panel 3: THAT'S NOT HOW IT ENDS. / OH, YEAH, THEN THERE'S THE TOW TRUCK.

Panel 1: PRESIDENT RAT / I KNOW A LOT OF YOU DIDN'T THINK I'D BE A SERIOUS PRESIDENT. THAT I'D BE TOO DISTRACTED BY PETTY CONCERNS.

Panel 2: WELL, I'M NOT. IN MY FIRST 100 DAYS, I WILL TAKE ON ALL THE BIG ISSUES FACING THIS COUNTRY.

Panel 3: WHAT FIRST, SIR? / NO MORE PINEAPPLE ON PIZZA.

Panel 4: I SEE. / EATING IT WILL BE A FELONY.

Just a day or so after this strip appeared, the president of Iceland made news by announcing he wanted to ban pineapple on pizza. Was it just a coincidence? Does he read *Pearls*? I don't know.

I will go to any length to set up a pun. Need an electrician who also happens to be a Ding Dong snack cake? No problem.

245

OKAY, GOAT, TODAY IS THE DAY I TAKE PRECEDENCE OVER EVERYTHING ELSE IN YOUR LIFE.

AND WHY IS THAT?

PRECEDENCE DAY.

PRESIDENTS DAY.

OH, WHO WANTS TO CELEBRATE THEM?

HEY, RAT, WANT TO GO TO THE MOVIES WITH ME TODAY?

CAN'T. BUSY.

WHAT ARE YOU DOING?

FINDING EVERYONE WHO ENDS THEIR SOCIAL MEDIA POSTS WITH "JUST SAYIN'" AND BEATING THEM OVER THE HEAD.

THAT'S GONNA BE A BUSY DAY.

HAHA, YEAH... JUST SAY—

CRACK

Rat has a point.

Just sayin'.

HOW'S IT GOING, BIOLOGIST BOB?

GOOD. BEEN DOING A LOT OF GENETIC RESEARCH ON CHIMPS. IT'S HELPFUL 'CAUSE AS A HUMAN, I SHARE 99% OF THEIR GENES.

LIES.

WHY DO YOU SAY THAT?

BECAUSE YOU COULD NEVER FIT INTO THEIR LITTLE PANTS.

YOU'RE WHY SCIENTISTS ARE ANTI-SOCIAL.

AND WHAT MONKEY EVEN WANTS YOUR FRUMPY OLD DAD JEANS?

We really do share 99 percent of our genes with chimps. Which is hard for me to believe when they can swing from everything and I can't do a pull-up.

That's nothing compared to an item you sometimes find at state fairs: a fried stick of butter. The food label just says, "You will die very soon."

I have a friend who does this "two-ish" thing. You never have any idea when he's gonna show up.

'IF ALL OF LIFE WAS LIKE FLYING COACH.'

I BASED IT ON PERSONAL EXPERIENCE.

HAVE SIX PEANUTS!

My wife brushes her teeth all the time and has many cavities. I brush once a day and have very few. Kids, this proves that brushing your teeth is stupid.

For those who don't know the reference, Rat's line in the last panel is something Al Pacino's character, Michael Corleone, says to his brother Fredo before he has him killed in a boat on Lake Tahoe.

I read a lot of history. And the most incompetent, arrogant loser I have ever read about is General George McClellan. He thought he was the second coming of Napoleon, but in truth, he was an incompetent blowhard. If you've never read about him, you should. His letters to his wife are comedy gold.

Sometimes, when I'm really bored, I will ride those little mechanical horses you see outside grocery stores. They're not that fun.

Weird Comics Page Fact: You can say "hell" if it's a reference to a place (for example, "There's a heaven and there's a hell"). But if you say something like "to hell with you" or "hell no," you're in trouble.

When I was a lawyer, I once left an entire file on top of my car and drove off. This may be why I'm no longer a lawyer.

This mini-golf course was going to be a whole series, but for some reason I stopped after just a couple days.

"Plethora" really is the most overused word by people trying to show they are smart. I could cite a plethora of examples.

I was sort of surprised I got away with this one. But that really is what Brits call an eraser.

And with that, another treasury is concluded. But before you go, please be sure to turn the page and give me your honest opinion.

Now It's
Your Turn

I'm a firm believer that the only way to get better as a cartoonist is to get feedback from your readers.

You have to know which characters resonate, what kinds of jokes are the best liked, and what readers want to see more of.

To have that dialogue is very important. And it works best when fans are encouraged to be open, honest, and detailed about their preferences. Because in the end, that creates a much better comic strip.

So on the next page, you'll find two postcards. If you have a minute, just fill them out, add postage, and mail them in.

And I'll strive to incorporate all of your feedback.

Thanks a lot,

Stephan